DR. AI

Sleeping with a Stranger

The Life You Did Not Plan

Sleeping with a Stranger: The Life You Did Not Plan
Copyright 2020 © Dr. Ann Jones, IAM Harvest Network
PO Box 143097, Fayetteville, GA 30214

ISBN 978-0-578-24264-4

Printed in the United States of America

S*leeping with a Stranger* is so near and dear to our family's hearts. We all physically walked through this dementia journey with my daddy. Never in a million years did I think we would experience something so painful as a family. My daddy was my hero. He was our savior. He always made everything alright. He was our security, our provider, and our caretaker. Then, we found him needing all of the above from us, his family.

The one thing I discovered on this journey with my daddy was that God truly does step in when we feel like we can't do it. For the last six years of my dad's life, we lost another piece of him daily. I would cry often just wishing I could talk to him and get his advice. I would see it in his eyes as he was losing his thoughts. He would play it off so well. I watched as my sweet angel of a mama had to step in and become the head of the home while making sure my daddy still felt like the king of his castle. Though this was the hardest thing I have ever walked through, it brought us together as a family. Each one of us, including my sons, stepped in to take the best care of our dad. God proved himself over and over to us. He allowed us to keep my daddy at home instead of admitting him to a nursing home. He kept his dignity to the very last breath.

I discovered in this journey what an insanely anointed writer my mama is. She has a way of painting a picture with her words that bring you into the very moment. I believe that her writing actually kept her sane. This book, *Sleeping with a Stranger*, is for anyone walking through their own hell. It doesn't matter if it's a divorce or infidelity or even a bankruptcy, addiction or sickness. This book will help you navigate and even escape a moment of your own reality to live in ours. If God can do it for our family then He will do it for you and yours. This book will guide you and reinstall hope for your next season. Your next is connected to your now. Whatever you are going through is going to be a part of your bestseller that God is creating through you in this journey of life.

My prayer is that while you read this, your heart strengthens and my sweet mama's words begin to bring you life. That you begin to see that, as long as you have a pulse, God still has a plan. This is a season in your life, not a sentence. That this is a moment, not a monument. What God has for you is for YOU. His promises never ever change, no matter where you find yourself today.

I watched as my mom so gracefully walked through this most devastating long season with my dad, and she is going to give you answers you need to make it through whatever you need to get through, whatever mountain you are staring at today. This book *Sleeping with a Stranger* is your trajectory shift.

I love you, Mom. I am so proud of you. You put your heart, soul and many tears into this book. You dignified dementia and honored our dad in such a beautiful way. Watching you whisper to him the day he took his last breath, "Henry, serving you these last fifty-two years has been my greatest assignment," changed me forever. I want to be like you when I grow up, my angel on earth.

Your Daughter, *Kimberly*
(Real Talk Kim)

*S*leeping with a Stranger is the unforgettable journey of a man and a woman who loved each other for 52 years of wedded bliss. They also happen to be my father and mother. This book, a labor of love, written by my mother is the story of her serving my father in the darkest days of his life.

It is the story of a woman and a man who lived the nightmare called dementia. My father was the strongest man I knew and led our family through many ups and downs in life. He allowed God to use him in a mighty way around the world for fifty plus years of ministry before his health began to fail. He escaped a life of poverty and by the grace of God found a destiny that afforded his family the greatest of lives. I'm so grateful to have been counted worthy to be called his son.

The woman, I affectionately call Mom, is one of the strongest women that I know. She is my hero and I'm so very proud of all that she has accomplished with her life. My favorite season by far, and there were many, was the season of watching her selflessly serve my dad with unconditional love. In this book she shares that journey and shows the way to live the life that Jesus calls us to live, a life of serving one another.

To some she is Mimi, to some she is friend, to others she is pastor, but to me she is a superwoman that has proven over and over again, this life is what you choose to make of it. In the pages of this book, you will discover the secret to stepping into your best life even when it seems too overwhelming to continue on. As Winston Churchill so famously expressed, "Never Give Up, Never Give Up!" Sit back and enjoy the journey, *"Sleeping with a Stranger."*

Henry and Ann's son, *Rob*
(Pastor Rob Jones)

Table of Contents

Acknowledgements   1

Introduction   3

PART 1   *Awakening*

Chapter 1   Disconnected by Dementia   9
            Questions, Questions and More Questions

Chapter 2   He left, But I Stayed   19
            Who Had This Man Become?

Chapter 3   Easy Decisions are Hard to Make   29
            There are No Guarantees

Chapter 4   But We are Pastors   37
            The Journey is Never Easy

            _____

PART 2   *Revelation*

Chapter 5   It's Easy to be Angry and Hard to Understand   45
            The Last 'I Love You'

Chapter 6   Meet the Joneses   55
               Just Ordinary People

Chapter 7   Miracles, Signs and Wonders   63
               It's a Faith Walk

Chapter 8   But Did it Kill You   71
               Equipped to Endure Hard Times

PART 3   Transformation

Chapter 9   This Too Shall Pass   85
               Storms Do Run Out of Rain

Chapter 10   Mourn and Move   91
               Just One Step at a Time

Chapter 11   52 Years, 3 Months, 6 Days   97
               Journey of a Lifetime

Chapter 12   How in the World Do You Move On?   107
               Just Get Up One More Day

Acknowledgements

First, I would like to give glory to God for what He has done! My heart is full of thanksgiving and all praise goes to Jesus Christ for walking with me through this season of writing!

I realize I could never have completed this project without my wonderful family, son, Rob, daughter, Kimberly, daughter-in-love, Melissa, and five grandsons, Morgan, Robey and Dakota, Lyncoln, Peyton and Cameron; you guys are my total support system. Rob and Kimberly, you two were the most amazing son and daughter throughout your lifetime; however, during the last few months of your dad's life you made me proud. Watching you not only bathe and change him but love on him as though it would be your last totally wrecked me many times.

Morgan, there are many days that I could not have continued to support your Papa at home if you had not been my constant support. Not one time did you refuse me when I needed your assistance. Even after working through the night, you still were on call whenever needed. I will never forget your love and honor.

To the memory of my amazing best friend, mentor and husband of fifty-two years, Dr. Henry R. Jones. It could not have happened without our journey together.

I'd like to say thank you also to our spiritual sons and daughters who have always believed in our vision and the call of God on our lives as a spiritual father and mother.

Lastly, I will always be thankful for Jennifer Hudson, who is such a comfort when needed and my BFF for eighteen years and counting.

Introduction

If you had told me, at twenty-years of age, that my life journey would look as it does, I would have immediately determined that I was getting off the roller coaster of life and choosing an easier path.

Born into a family who had lived on the same land for one hundred years, I could never have dreamed that I would have traveled around the world many times and lived away from our home state of North Carolina our entire marriage. My dream as a young girl was the same story, I think most girls dream – that little house with a handsome husband, a son and daughter and the white picket fence.

How I ended up with my family and life's possessions crowded into a small travel trailer and then moved from state to state in revival followed by the planting of churches was outside my comfort zone. Yet, God was a good father. As I rehearse my life's journey, I realize how good He was as He navigated our journey. I had no idea that dementia would partner with us the last five years of our lives and eventually steal my man from me.

Hang on as you traverse my life with me! You will see that we absolutely were not perfect, we did not have the answers to every life challenge and yet, God was there in every situation!

You will see that the most important prayer we prayed was that God would show Himself mighty through us, and we would show His love to His people as He does. My Henry always had certain faith quotes that he used in his conversations so you will understand as each chapter is introduced by one of his famous quotes which he had adopted throughout his life journey.

Please do one thing with me as you begin my journey with me. Pray this prayer that has kept me on my feet and moving the last five years of my life:

"Dear Lord Jesus, in every decision I make today, please conform me to your image. Allow me to be that light that someone sees today. I invite you to be Lord of every area of my life – my spirit, soul, body, heart, mind and will. Be Lord of my home, my household, my finances, and every decision that I make will be filtered through the Holy Spirit. Amen."

PART 1

awakening

It's no hill for a climber.

one
Disconnected by Dementia

Questions, Questions and More Questions

ow could this brilliant man who was a walking Bible become a victim in our story? Dr. Henry R. Jones was a man's man who was honored and respected by all those who called him pastor, apostle, prophet and friend. He commanded your attention when he walked in the room without even expressing a word yet would give his entire focus when you spoke because he knew the importance of listening. As a counselor to ministry, he would spend hours with those in ministry who had flown in just to receive of his knowledge in the deliverance of the spirit, soul and body. The dreaded disease of dementia that had attacked his dad, his aunt and his uncle was now knocking on his door. After the fact, I now know that dementia is a general term for the loss of memory and other cognitive abilities serious enough to alter the face of an entire family.

When Henry, my husband of forty-seven years, was diagnosed in February 2015, with early onset dementia, we had no idea that more than five million Americans have Alzheimer's, the most common form of dementia. Even though his dad, aunt and uncle died from Alzheimer's, it was forty years ago when his dad passed.

We were thirty years of age and busy building a new church in West Point, Mississippi. When Henry received a distressed call letting him know that his dad was hospitalized and failing quickly, Henry immediately flew to Burlington, North Carolina to see his dad before he passed. As he stepped into his dad's room, his dad seemed to rally again as though he might have recognized him. It was the exact type of reaction that Henry needed at that time; yet, the next six days, he watched his dad wrestle with pneumonia and other health issues.

After receiving a call from home from the building crew, Henry knew he needed to get back to supervising the church building project. Upon arriving home, he received the dreaded call that his dad had passed after having a heart attack. Henry was distraught that his dad was gone. I can still remember the anguish of the funeral, even today. How in the world could a disease totally rob you of your loved one years before he even passed? Why could we not have had many more years to enjoy the relationship of family?

Then, we resumed our life as usual. We were busy just very busy people living, raising our two children, building churches, revivals. We started to make newer and happier memories, so, the distress of this dreaded disease was filed away in our memory banks.

Major Scare

Our life had been so full and exciting. Together we were traveling to the nations, building and pastoring churches, mentoring pastors. Then, one afternoon in June of 2011, Henry and I were returning home from Atlanta when he began to experience the symptoms of a heart attack. Immediately I took the wheel and drove to the physician's office where an EKG was done. Because it looked normal, the physician sent Henry to the cardiologist for a second opinion. Although the cardiologist had the same opinion as the primary care physician, Henry was scheduled the next morning for a heart catherization. During the heart catherization, I was informed that they had found four blockages, so they were transporting him to a hospital in the city for stents. Thankfully, the surgery went well, and my honey was able to come home the next day.

The surgeon had informed us that Henry would need to give up his much-loved Breyer's vanilla bean ice cream/coffee floats which he had secretly been drinking each week for the last year while I was at church in music practice. I had no idea that this man would rush to the grocery store as soon as I departed the house to purchase his beloved ice cream. He would then brew his coffee and mix his floats, one after the other, until he had finished the one-half gallon of ice cream. The surgeon was able to awaken him to the necessity of total abstinence because of the butter fat in the ice cream. I thought if I had given my husband an ultimatum as the surgeon did that day, he, being the strong controller that he was, would have laughed at me and let me know the ice cream certainly wasn't hurting him.

Of course, later my grandsons laughingly informed me that, when their papa would take them out for an outing, they headed straight for Dairy Queen for their much needed chocolate shake. So, you see, I knew that it must be our prayers that kept my hubby going because he was truly a connoisseur of anything sweet.

Life seemed to be back to normal. One year later, I began to notice that Henry was having memory problems. One afternoon he was visiting a pastor friend at a nursing home about fifteen miles away. I received a frantic phone call from Henry saying he could not find his way home. I immediately jumped into action – went to the computer to see where the nursing home was located. I then began asking him for landmarks of his location. Honestly, I have no idea how in the world I was able to direct him home that day. I think, that started a series of instances that made me realize something was wrong. Looking back at those early days of the onset of memory loss, I am so very thankful that we were able to eventually download the iPhone app, Life 360, to keep our family connected.

During his annual follow-up appointment with the cardiologist, I explained that life was changing at home. Henry would forget simple things. Today, this seems so menial; however, I am talking about a man who was a walking Bible who knew thousands of scriptures, who could give me locations for any verses that I recited and took care of every area of our lives.

This man would sit upstairs in his office for hours online managing our finances, taxes and everyday bill paying. Before online bill-paying was popular, Henry was already paying taxes and all monthly bills online. I had no idea his procedures until he traveled alone to the nation of Indonesia in 2011 for nineteen days. He left the instructions on how to process our bills and taxes while he was out of the country; however, I was a nervous wreck. I had never had to use usernames and passwords for paying our monthly bills. Why in the world could I not just write checks and send by mail like most of the population? That was my question every day that he was gone. Yet this man was always progressive and had changed our entire system, so I had to move into the twenty-first century while he was traveling the world.

THERE WERE MORE QUESTIONS THAN ANSWERS!

I still remember the feelings of anxiety as I would enter my username and password to go online to pay bills. What if I messed up and was in someone else's account? What if I entered the wrong payment? I cannot tell you how many times I contacted him even though he was ten thousand miles and a totally different time zone from me. Thank God he was patient as I learned this new process. I wonder now if he had a premonition of our life as it would become. I had never worried about our household budget nor even the church's budget because he had always been the bottom line. He was now letting me know I was well able to move into this next season.

Dr. Henry R. Jones, as he was known until the end of his life, was a man's man. He worked hard and played hard. He could sit across the desk of the local bank manager and explain his vision for a new church building without breaking a sweat. More than once, in disbelief, our church board would wait for him to return from a crucial financial meeting knowing there was no way the bank would release funds to our little struggling congregation to keep building, and yet, he would walk in with the funds to build another floor.

So, how in the world could this brilliant man who had more common sense than any human being I had ever met arrive at the point of being unsettled about everything in life? What was it about this horrendous disease that would turn a man's man who took care of everyone into a frail man needing his wife to even feed him if he was going to eat? I am still amazed that I did not question the God that I served who had created this entire universe why my husband was walking out the family curse which had attacked so many family members.

Unsure of our Journey

We began this journey not understanding where we were headed. In fact, Henry would not accept that he had been dealt this awful sickness. He would tell his family that he would not receive this illness. He had broken the family curse of Alzheimer's, so there was no way he would have it. He had begun taking vitamins and herbs in his twenties. I can tell you that, at most times, our house looked like an herb shop. People would call him for answers to their health challenges as he was a health researcher. Yet, I lived with him. I watched him gradually begin to lose his ability to process simple actions. No, it did not happen overnight. Thank God for that.

In fact, thank God that we have many videos showing the process of loss. The times he would get so angry because he just could not figure things out. He would walk through the house while rearranging everything in his path. Truly, I would miss vases, pictures, even fruit from my table. I would question everything missing until I knew there was nothing he could do. He just would not remember what he had done with anything. He had even begun collecting ball point pens. After his death, as we were sorting his clothes, Rob and I found pens in jacket and pant pockets. In fact, anywhere he could keep a collection of pens became his hiding place.

When you are faced with an illness in your family, you realize that you just keep living. You just keep coping and doing those things necessary that keeps everything flowing in the family.

For the first two years, Henry did so well that we were all encouraged. I would listen to holistic neurologists for hours online and order every type of vitamin and herb they recommended to feed the brain. The first nutrition we started taking was the coconut oil. I would buy jars of organic coconut oil and my little husband would take huge spoonsful of the oil along with numerous vitamins. You see, the coconut oil feeds the brain, so I was told. Today, after the fact, I still believe that this is a super healthy food so will always use coconut oil in my cooking.

When the neurologist became part of our lives in 2015, he did what all neurologists do. He prescribed Aricept and then Namenda I can tell you that I never saw any results from these two medications. In fact, I researched everything that was given to him and never found that the results were favorable. I realize today that the doctors do not have the answer for this disease that is rampant around the world.

I began asking questions and reading anything I could find on Alzheimer's since that was the word most familiar to me. I had no idea that Alzheimer's accounts for 60 to 80 percent of all dementia cases. I really thought dementia was a form of Alzheimer's. Today, I realize there are all types of dementia such as Vascular dementia, Mixed dementia, Parkinson's disease dementia, Dementia with Lewy bodies, Huntington's disease dementia, Creutzfeldt-Jakob disease, Frontotemporal dementia, Normal pressure hydrocephalus and even Down syndrome dementia. These are just a few of the types, so you can now understand why people are not understanding the magnitude of this dreaded disease.

Because Alzheimer's is the most common form, I want you to understand why this disease can change the entire face of a family. The brain has 100 billion nerve cells, and each cell has a purpose. These brain cells operate like tiny factories. They receive supplies, generate energy, construct equipment and get rid of waste. Scientists believe that these diseases associated with dementia prevent different cells from doing what they were made to do. The scientists are not sure, even today, where the trouble starts. Just like in a real factory, backups and breakdowns in one system cause problems in other areas. As damage spreads, cells lose their ability to do their jobs and, eventually, die.

Though autopsy studies show that most people develop some plaques and tangles as they age, those with the diseases connected to dementia tend to develop far more and develop them in a predictable pattern, beginning in the areas important for memory before spreading to other regions.

The sad fact is that scientists do not know exactly what role plaques and tangles play in this disease. The destruction and death of nerve cells causes memory failure, personality changes, and problems in carrying out daily activities.

The diagnosis we received on that fateful day in February 2015, was early onset dementia. It was enough to shake my very foundation. The first thing the doctor did upon arrival was give my husband the common test – draw a clock, insert numbers, and then he asked him to draw in a certain time. Henry did well to draw the circle for the clock. He could not figure out where the numbers were supposed to go. I cannot tell you how many times I have drawn this clock to just assure myself that I am doing well. The doctor then asked the name of our president, the year, our address and Henry's birthday.

Facing Year-End Exams

For the first appointment, I felt like I was facing year-end exams in school as I was tutoring Henry on the way to the doctor. What is your birthday? Henry, what is your address? Do you know our president? He really could answer these if he was prompted. I was a good prompter. When the neurologist would begin asking questions, Henry would immediately look in my direction. So, the doctor would excuse me so he could be alone with my husband. So, every six months, the same procedure. Can you name the president, what is the year and your address?

After our first visit, Henry was driving us home and I was in my own world of disbelief. I refused to fall apart. I kept talking to myself to keep it together. I knew I had to call my son, Rob, and daughter, Kimberly, to inform them of the diagnosis. I knew I could not do it without falling apart, so I waited until we arrived home.

Even though the doctor had said that Henry would need to give up driving, I could not figure life as it was going to be. How in the world would I tell this strong man who was behind the wheel, if the car was moving, that he could no longer drive? He was the one who ran to the grocery story several times a day for things that I had forgotten yet needed for baking. How would I survive without him? There were more questions than answers.

DISCONNECTED BY DEMENTIA

Why worry about tomorrow?
It does not rob tomorrow of its
sorrow; it only saps today of
its strength.

two

He Left, But I Stayed

Who Had This Man Become?

could never have dreamed that the long conversations we had enjoyed together as we traveled throughout the world would eventually become one-word answers. Even the day he began instructing me on the online bill paying was a revelation of what our future would be. Then one day, we stepped into the garage and he decided he no longer wanted to drive. He wanted me to take my place on the driver's side. I had been dreading this moment for months and could not have dreamed how easily we transitioned that day. Maybe all the transitions through this dreaded disease would be so easy. This was my conversation with myself that day. I can tell you that I could never have imagined the countless days of trying to figure life out because there is no formula for families traversing this horrendous disease.

Who in the world was this man that I was living with that I still called my husband? Henry Jones was always behind the wheel of any automobile in which he was riding. He was a GPS before GPS became familiar to the world. When we arrived in Atlanta in 1979, I was amazed how quickly he became familiar with the city streets and every hospital represented. We did not use maps and yet, he could drive to any location. Of course, there were a few times in our marriage when he would rather drive one hundred miles out of the way than admit he had missed it. I would be heavily suggesting that he stop and ask directions; however, this man would never admit he did not know his location. He would keep driving until we miraculously arrived at the very business or hospital or church in which we were headed. You know how it is. You cannot tell a man that he's wrong. Finally, I understood our dynamic. He was the head and I learned to be the neck that turned the head. What is amazing is that Henry jokingly let everyone know that I was the force behind the scene.

WHO WAS THIS MAN I WAS LIVING WITH?

So, as we faced one more crisis together, I truly believed that, in this journey of dementia that we were facing, we would win in the end. I did not know what the final end would be, but I knew we had never faced crises alone. As much as I wanted to believe that Henry would survive one more life challenge, I could never have written this final chapter until it was over.

I knew my entire life that Henry was God's answer to my prayer for a husband that I would live with until death do us part. You see, growing up in a home where my mother was one more strong-willed human being, and my dad made sure our world centered around her, I decided that I wanted a man who could stand up for himself because I knew as much as I suffered from insecurity and low self-esteem, I was still a force to be reckoned with. I knew my stubbornness was something that I would need to curtail if I wanted to make a marriage not just survive but thrive. Please don't misunderstand me. My dad was a saint in my eyes. He was a true man of God who would have gladly laid his life down for our family.

The Kellum family had the perfect family dynamic with three kids and a dog until my baby brother, Randy, passed away at two years of age. It was one of those unforeseen family tragedies that changes the total dynamic of a family for an entire lifetime. My brother, Rodney, was nine years of age and I was seven the week Randy became ill. He had had a bout with the measles several weeks before and seemed to be doing great. However, my mom would have me entertain him inside the house while they would work in the garden. I still remember us standing on the couch while looking out the window, two little minions wanting to be outside.

Now, this baby was like the focus of our world. Even my dad loved him with an unexplainable love because this little two-year-old would stand on the seat by my dad and wrap his arm around my dad's shoulders as he drove. Randy seemed to connect with my dad like no one else. Even when my dad was preaching, Randy would disrupt the service by crying while Mom was holding him. Finally, Dad would walk down to the front pew, pick him up, sit him on the platform behind him, and this little character would be as happy as a kid with a lollipop. We all were amazed at his dedication to Dad.

So, when Randy became feverish one afternoon, we all were loaded into the family car and headed to the doctor's. He checked Randy and then sent us to the hospital. Randy was admitted that night, and that was the last time I saw my sweet angel alive. Two days later, he succumbed to meningitis, and I remember it today as though it just happened.

Through the Eyes of a Child

He died on Thursday, and his body was brought to our house in a small casket on Friday. In those days, it was customary to bring the deceased family member home for the wake. Remember, I was seven years old. My mother became so distraught that the doctor prescribed medication to assist her in sleeping. Of course, all she wanted to do was sleep to numb the pain, so I would walk from room to room just needing someone to hold me. No one was there. Everyone was trying to help comfort my family; however, it was as if I did not exist. I always felt like I lost my sweet little baby brother and my mother at the same time.

This tragedy caused my mom to begin a spiral into the dark world of mental illness. She would keep herself so medicated to not feel loss while unable to exist in the real world. The next two years were a blur in my memories until my mom became pregnant with my new baby sister. Now listen, when that little baby girl arrived, I thought I had a new baby doll. However, my mom would not even look at her in the hospital because she wasn't a boy. She had prayed that God would give her a boy to take Randy's place. Now, we know that would never have worked out for the good for a little boy to have been raised in the shadow of his deceased brother. God totally knew what was best for our family. While in the hospital, everyone was trying to coach my mom into holding her new baby. She declared she would not look at that little baby girl nor hold her.

Finally, a day later, the doctor gave my mother an ultimatum. Just take a look at Pamela Kay and then, if she decided she could not accept her, the doctor explained that he would gladly adopt this beautiful child. Of course, this was a ploy by the doctor because he knew that just a look would change my mother's heart. So, my mother agreed to at least look. When Pamela was brought into her room, the staff had dressed her like a little princess. She had the most gorgeous headful of black hair and blue eyes. I, of course, was smitten. I would have fought anyone if they had tried to take her away from our family. My mother immediately fell in love with this little bundle of joy, so, yes, my sister went home with us that day.

WHERE IN THE WORLD COULD THIS WOMAN BE HIDING?

Not sure how it happened, but I became the one who rocked her to sleep every night. Oh, and I also had to sing her a lullaby. Even those nights when I had been outside playing and was exhausted for an eight-year-old, I knew my duty was to rock my baby to sleep. The reason I even tell this story is because that little girl is now a sixty-four-year-old who has been brightening up the world of anyone she has met throughout her lifetime. She is one of the most talented musicians that I know and would give her shirt to anyone that needed it. She also became the caregiver for my mom the last three years of her life. This is an important part of our story because we both learned to walk in forgiveness with our mom before she went to her forever home.

You see, we had no idea that we had carried so much pain throughout our lifetime. How can you live a life of service in ministry, pastoring churches, and not understand that you could carry abandonment issues and resentment for having such an irregular family? By the way, we also have a brother, Ricky, born three years after Pamela, and I always felt so sad that they had never lived in our home when it seemed to be perfect. Truly, before Randy died, I know we probably had financial issues and sickness, the normal type of challenges that every family face. However, after the death, we were never normal again.

Mom tried to work outside the home, but many times, she would lose consciousness at work and need to be taken to the hospital. We had no idea it was anxiety. I remember even the graveside service for my grandmother. While the family walked by the casket to view my grandmother one last time, my mother passed out. The funeral director immediately placed a paper bag over her head so she could get some oxygen. Honestly, that frightened me more than my mother laying over my dead grandmother. So, we realized that we would need to keep paper bags available to assist when my mother would have an anxiety attack. Who had heard of anxiety attacks that could cripple a family that many years ago? It would be so normal now, but I can tell you we were anything but normal.

My dad worked hard as a carpenter to provide for our family and take care of Mom. So many times, I was the delegated caregiver while he was working or away preaching. Anyway, my brother and sister were too young for that amount of responsibility. I remember one Sunday when my dad was to be away all day, so I was instructed to stay at home to keep Mom safe. Dad took Rick and Pamela with him, so it was just Mom and me. The closer it got to church time, I thought, "Mom's not going anywhere. She is passed out on the bed, sedated. Why not go to church for one hour and then rush back home?" So, I did. What could it hurt?

I was miserable at church because fear takes the fun out of anything. As I raced into the house to check on Mom, I glanced in her bedroom where she was always asleep. Except this day. Where in the world could this woman who never leaves her house be hiding? My heart was racing as I ran from room to room screaming as loud as possible. Finally, back to her room. Not in her bathroom. Even today, I cannot imagine why I looked under the bed. Yes, there she was, soundly asleep. I think she had tried to get up to go the bathroom, fell and ended up under the bed. You do know that I did not tell my dad what had happened. He would have killed me. Not literally but I would have wanted to be dead.

Mental Illness

Because I blamed all the medications for not having a mom, one day when I was sixteen years of age, I grabbed a bag and filled it up with all Mom's meds. I figured if she did not have them, she could not take them and be overmedicated all the time. However, when my dad came home from work, he wanted to know where her meds were hidden. Do you know that I never told him? He begged me to return the meds so he could give them to her. I would not do it because I knew she would get better if she did not have all the meds. Of course, this was immaturity thinking that I knew what was best. You see, it wasn't the meds that had made her sick. It was a mental illness.

During this troubling time, my mom had three nervous breakdowns, and we would escort her to a mental hospital called Dix Hill one hundred miles from our house. Each time we dropped Mom at that facility, it was as though she died another death. However, when we would pick her up after a few weeks of being clean, it was as though our family was normal again. We knew as we drove toward the hospital that everything would be alright. And it was for a short while. Then Mom would begin going to all the doctors and mental health clinics again. They would prescribe her more medication and then we would start losing her all over again.

During my senior year in high school, I had perfect attendance until Mom's birthday. She was in the hospital, and we were going to take a picnic and eat with her on the grounds at the mental hospital. It was a toss-up for me. Would Mom know me? Would it be worth my time to go and lose my perfect attendance? Isn't it sad that such a trivial thing could drive a teen because my life had been so abnormal that all I wanted was a little normalcy.

Normalcy was winning awards at school, becoming president of clubs, even driving a school bus in high school. I would get so frustrated because I could not talk to my mom about these things. Even though I was popular in school, I would not date because I was embarrassed because of my home situation. Finally, at seventeen years of age, I began dating a young man. The weird thing is that Mom seemed to get so much better during this time. My friend and I had a normal dating relationship, and he would even come in to pick me up. Before this time, I did not want anyone to know we had sickness in our home.

It's so amazing to me now how I could be embarrassed that my mom was sick. Would I have felt the same way if it had been cancer or diabetes? It was as though mental illness was the plague or something as horrendous. You know, I realize now that the homelife I had experienced set me up to be a caregiver who would serve others throughout my lifetime. Instead of living a life of resentment, it was as though I had been trained to think of others before myself. Maybe it was because I had cared for my brother and sister like a mother would. Maybe it was because I had watched my dad be the greatest caregiver I could have ever imagined. All I know is that in my teen years, before I met the love of my life, I could never have imagined that I would become his caregiver until my Henry drew his last breath.

Honestly, no one can give you a day-to-day formula as you traverse life's tragedies. I am a living testimony that, when I did not have any answers, God still came through for me. I would pick up the right brochure or meet someone at the grocery store who would give me direction for that day. I have always testified that, when I don't know what to do, God will make me to know His direction. I had lived with my honey for fifty-two years as he directed our lives together and kept us on track. Then, gradually, life began evolving into a day-by-day list of duties as I awakened to assist my gorgeous man in getting him up for the day. He was unable to even arise for the day without assistance. In fact, Henry did not drink or eat without assistance, so I made sure I would stay focused on his needs for the day. That was my priority.

You don't realize where life is taking you until you are there and yet, you tell yourself that you are walking by faith and not by sight. I can tell you that I am an example of God's grace after my honey passed from such a horrendous disease, and yet I have not lost my faith. Henry, who always let everyone know that his name meant ruler of an estate, could never have dreamed that he would sit hour after hour while waiting on others to make all the decisions concerning his life. He always called himself a mover and a shaker because, if it could be done, Henry would accomplish it. And then, the last ten months of his life, he was housebound and depended on everyone to take care of every menial task from bathing to dressing to feeding.

Even on that fateful day in February 2015, when Henry and I received the dreaded diagnosis of early onset dementia, there were no special instructions on how you can recoup the days you lose nor the sleepless nights as life progressively gets worse. The only instructions given to us by the neurologist on that fateful day was to do what you've always planned on doing – take a cruise or a much needed vacation. What is amazing is we did take that cruise to Honduras and loved every minute of it. Do our family have memories worth a million dollars that will sustain us through our lifetime? Absolutely! We took lots of pictures and videos and savored each day as though it would be our last until it was.

When you're born in the fire,
you can't live in the smoke.

three

Easy Decisions are Difficult to Make

There are No Guarantees

Even though you do nothing to deserve dementia, you still feel as though you could have done things differently. You begin questioning the way you ate, exercised, even lived that could have made a difference. You then must determine the simple actions that will make life easier for your loved one.

As I write, I realize it's been 7.429 weeks or 52 days or 1,248 hours or 74,880 minutes or 4,492,800 seconds since my best friend soared to his forever home. Many people live in the element of time and have allowed this time to totally take over their very existence. While talking with a friend, I was told that, even though their loved one had passed six years ago, they were still trying to deal with the loss.

I had suffered loss in my life previously and could show empathy for other's loss; however, when Henry passed, I was thrown into a new category called *widow*. It was a week after that momentous passing that I realized I was now alone and yet I wasn't. Yes, I have a son, Rob, and daughter, Kimberly, but there's still those night hours when no one is lying beside you and you become enveloped in aloneness.

What more could I have done? I spent hundreds of dollars, maybe thousands, on nutrition to feed Henry's brain. I even went to the extent of hiring a nutritionist to put us on a schedule of foods and nutrition that would give healing to a brain that was already being ravaged by a disease in which the specialists had no answer.

I have watched the world bow down to COVID 19, this unknown virus that attacks people anytime, anywhere. No one knows the origin or solution to bringing this unknown enemy to its knees. This virus, or whatever it's called, has totally affected every area of our lives. It has devasted world economies and entire nations. When we think an end is coming, we then hear that a new surge is on its way, so people stay suspended in time while not knowing how to break out and begin living again.

This sounds like the life I have been living for the last five years with Henry who was such a force in our family that we all just listened and moved when he spoke. So, we now live in the before and after. Remember, we did this before – Cancun and Hawaii vacations, cruises, church plants, revivals, and, of course, traveling the world.

After Henry was diagnosed, we traveled once more to Indonesia because we could. This nation was Henry's love, after God, his family, his nation. I'm not sure how in the world this nation was the one chosen. Henry had been to Honduras, Santo Domingo, Philippines, Amsterdam, and so many other places on missions' trips; however, when we traveled to Indonesia in 1997, it so affected Henry that we spent the next eighteen years in and out of that nation ministering to thousands.

I think one of the most exciting people that we met on our journeys through Indonesia was our friend, Harry Soetantyo, who scheduled our meetings to keep us on track as we traveled through the second largest nation in the world and the largest Muslim nation. People jokingly let us know through the years that we had preached in more cities in Indonesia than the permanent residents had even visited. We accounted all of this to Harry because he always scheduled us well.

WE DID NOT REALIZE THE IMPACT WE WERE MAKING!

Before we would leave the states, Harry would send us a tentative schedule which kept changing even after we arrived. When pastors, business owners and even families would hear that we were in Indonesia, Harry would laughingly let us know that he could schedule no one else at that time because we were so busy. When we first went to Indonesia, we thought everyone was as busy as we were. We would somedays speak three and four times daily and Sundays, at least five times.

Finally, Harry realized we needed days off also. Henry would be invited to play golf on some of the most gorgeous greens that we have ever seen because there were employees continually trimming the grass with small hand-held clippers. We were blessed to become friends with a man who owned most of the golf clubs throughout Indonesia and other nations, so Henry was invited to take a day off and just have fun. Of course, I loved him playing golf because that meant I had a shopping day.

I will always remember my friends, Diana and Lucille, who were my shopping mates. And by the way, did I tell you that the malls in Indonesia are the most amazing malls full of designer shops? You can find the latest and the greatest, the newest design of Gucci, Louis Vuitton,

Chanel, Fendi, and any other design you might want. However, they knew I loved to shop at Mangga Dua Mall. This shopping plaza fulfilled every girl's dream of what shopping heaven would look like. It reminded me of Americas Mart in Atlanta but much more reasonable in price.

My kids have called me cheap through the years because I love a deal and love to barter; however, I say that I am frugal. There is such a great difference between these two words. I do not mind spending money when necessary, but I love a great deal and will take extra time looking for that deal. My friends would tell me that, if they could not find the purse in the designer shop in which they were looking, they headed directly to Mangga Dua because they had the newest designer designs in knock offs. The amazing fact is you could not distinguish between the high-end knock offs and the real thing. You were even furnished with a bag and box to accompany that amazing purse or bag, as they called it.

A Time for Remembering

While I am in this time of remembering friends, I must give honor to my dear friend, Diana Tirtasaputra, who passed away with cancer last year. She was the most graceful human being with the sweetest spirit and biggest heart. It's difficult for me to take a journey down memory lane without mentioning the happy times we had shopping at Mangga Dua. Diana was an expert on Chanel so, on one of our trips, as we made our way through hundreds of little shops, floor after floor, searching for the right bag at the right price, Diana spotted a small Chanel leather black bag with a black shoulder chain. After much inspection, she whispered that she believed this could be the *real thing*. Here I am, a novice at shopping the *real thing*, so I totally believe what she said. She then asked to see the box and the bag. It all made a difference when shopping the *real thing*. The shop owner leaned over and quietly whispered to Diana that, sometimes there may be a small flaw in the *real thing* and so it may get sent out with knock offs. She declared this was a *real thing*, a true leather Chanel at a great price. So, I immediately jumped on that sale and came away with my prize of the day.

One year later, Diana and her family were in Atlanta visiting with us, and she wanted to shop Chanel. She wanted to find a purse much like the one that I had purchased in Indonesia. I was happy to give her our shopping experience. You know, it's amazing how we always feel like the grass is greener on the other side. They love our malls, and I love their malls. Diana did find a Chanel much like my style that day, and I was amazed at the price of the original compared to my token price that I had given at Mangga Dua. Hey, don't laugh at my frugality. I still have my Chanel bag, and it is still beautiful. And, yes, I do have several original designs that I have collected through the years, but who can tell?

FRIENDS HAD GIVEN HIM AN INDONESIAN NAME, DR. HENRI SUJONO.

The decision to travel to Indonesia one last time after Henry was diagnosed with dementia was difficult for me to make. I knew I would be taking care of him, watching out for him and covering him so others would not see that he was no longer the aggressive giant who could command your attention without even trying. Our Indonesian friends had even given him an Indonesian name through the years, Dr. Hendri Sujono. They honestly called him this so much that he would say this about himself. The Indonesian people would comment that they knew we loved their people, so they truly loved us. There were times through the years that we had to talk ourselves out of moving to that great nation. We had the responsibility of caring for my mother after my dad passed away. We had five handsome grandsons and their parents. We had our church and our network of churches.

I remember, on one occasion, when a pastor asked us to consider moving to Indonesia. He explained that we would be ministering in their churches throughout Indonesia but also throughout the world. He explained that he wanted me to go to a language school for six months to learn the language so I could be Henry's translator as he preached. The reason he even thought I could learn the language so quickly was because we sang songs in the Indonesia language and were told that our accent was so real that they knew I could also speak clearly.

Oh, how tempting this invitation was for us as we knew God had called us, in that season, to the Indonesian people. Yet, we knew that our responsibility at that time was taking care of my mom after my dad had passed. She had lived with us for years, and we knew we could never move to another nation and expect my sister to assume such a great responsibility. So, we had to decline the invitation that would have included housing, servants, cars and drivers throughout the nation. Even though we knew we had declined, when we arrived in the next city for ministry, we were greeted by many people so excited that we were moving from the U.S. We then were given the responsibility to explain our refusal – we dearly loved the people but knew God had us in the U.S. for this season.

It Would Have Been Easy to Say Yes

It would have been easy to say yes when asked to relocate to this amazing nation that was experiencing revival like we had never experienced. Henry always said that, when you were born in the fire, you cannot live in the smoke. He was a revivalist deep down in his being and would do whatever necessary to welcome the Holy Spirit no matter how many people were in attendance nor where we were ministering. So, when we arrived in Indonesia in January 1997, he stepped into an outpouring of revival unlike we had ever experienced. Not that we had not experienced revival, however, when you are ministering to 50,000 people on a Sunday, it totally gives you a spiritual rush like you have never experienced. Our Sundays would start at 5 a.m. or earlier as the first Sunday services were always very early and the largest of the day. This service would be followed by four or five more throughout the day.

Today as I travel with my daughter, Kimberly or Real Talk Kim as the world knows her, her ministry brings back memories of the days in Indonesia when, after ministering a service, an automobile would be waiting and you would be escorted immediately to the next service in another church in another part of the city. I love experiencing this today with Kimberly as she ministers to huge congregations in mega churches and then rushed to the next location. I am feeling right at home in the rush of evangelism.

I determined as Henry was progressing through the different stages of dementia that I would keep him totally immersed in church life, as much as possible. We look at different videos from our church today, and my honey, who was fighting with all his might to stay connected to the present, was dancing and enjoying the worship music while smiling as though he could not have been more excited. Whether Kimberly or Rob was ministering, he was letting those around us know that his kids were the best preachers, the best singers, just the best.

One of the most difficult times for me in the last stage, which lasted about ten months, before he had a massive seizure, was that he lost his ability to play the keyboard, guitar and organ. This man taught me to play the Hammond C3 organ, and he still outplayed me as long as he lived. I told you he was a revivalist. He believed you could not have a revival without a B3 or C3 Hammond. Until he moved into the seventh stage, he would walk around our house with his guitar picking and singing. He had even taught our first-born grandson, Morgan, guitar chords when he began developing a desire to play. Of course, after that, Morgan began watching YouTube videos and has become an accomplished guitarist and singer. You know, we totally believe in legacy.

It's tight but it's right.

four

But We are Pastors

The Journey is Never Easy

ementia may be a disease that you cannot dictate for your life, yet you still get embarrassed as you try to navigate life that is totally different than the life you had always lived. Pastoring a congregation and knowing that he, the man who had traveled the world numerous times speaking to congregations of thousands, now could only read his sermon because he could not put his thoughts together to sustain a message will cause you to begin trying to hide the fact that there is a disease invading his life. The problem was Henry would never accept that this awful disease that had incapacitated his dad, Henry R. Jones Sr., his Uncle Reuben and his Aunt Mary Lee could come calling at our door. His family was a family anointed for evangelism. In the fifties, his family of preachers filled tents with thousands and saw documented miracles and thousands of salvations. Numerous churches were founded and built because this family had determined that God would be first, and they would do His will.

Now, they were not a religious lot. What is amazing is that Aunt Mary Lee was the first one among the siblings to accept Jesus as Lord and then be filled with the Holy Spirit. The men in their family were moonshiners and even Henry's oldest brother hauled moonshine through the hills of North Carolina. Even Henry's grandfather died in prison because someone had shot the revenue officer who had found their liquor still. Henry's grandfather took the rap even though the family never believed he was the one who fired the shot. Does this sound like a preacher's family? Yet, when Aunt Mary Lee gave her heart to Jesus, she would not be quiet. She knew that her family needed God, and God had chosen her to be the one to begin revival. Even that is amazing to me as women were taught to keep silent and yet, this strong young woman took her stand and told her family what God had said. She would not take "No" for an answer and, by faith, knew God would bring her rowdy brothers to Him.

In fact, Henry's dad was a drunk until he was thirty-five years of age. I was told that he was being chased by some guys one Wednesday evening when he ducked into a little white church as the minister was preaching his sermon. Henry's dad fell asleep on the back row until the preacher had everyone stand and come down for prayer. His dad followed the little group of women and men as they went forward. I'm sure they sensed and smelled that he was drinking. They did not allow him to leave the altar that night until he had sobered up and accepted Jesus as Lord. Do you believe his dad made a total change in his life and never drank another drop of liquor? He became a preacher and, in fact, founded seven churches in North Carolina. His Uncle Reuben also became a preacher and began ministering in tents and tobacco warehouses. My mother and dad always talked about Sunday services under the big tents when thousands would be crowded together worshipping and seeing miracles happen.

Even though Henry and I did not officially meet until we were seventeen years of age, our parents worshipped together as revival fires blazed throughout the North Carolina countryside. My parents let me know that Henry and I had lain under the tent chairs as babies together. It is still amazing to me how, even though he lived two hundred miles away, we eventually met and knew there was an attraction. Three years after our first official meeting, we finally dated for a short period and then married.

I knew what I wanted

I knew when I was young that I wanted to be in full-time ministry. My parents, who were pastors, had raised me to love God and love His people. Yes, I experienced plenty of hurt dealing with church people because church people are just real people. However, it did not sway me from knowing that I was called to do more than just live life as usual. Even though I was an honor student in high school and had desired to go to college, I'm not sure why no one

HIS DAD NEVER DRANK ANOTHER DROP OF ALCOHOL!

had counseled me about seeking scholarships; however, I know that, if I had sought a college education at that time, Henry and I would not have been married at twenty years of age. I do know that God orders our steps, so I choose to believe that God's plan was our marriage and ministry. Of course, I was always and am still a student who loves to learn and challenged by growth. So, at thirty-five years of age, I began college to obtain a piano pedagogy degree. The amazing fact is that whatever I chose to pursue, Henry was my greatest supporter except when I would sit at the piano for hours practicing my runs and fills.

When I met Henry, he was an eligible young evangelist who had a group of young ladies following him to his revivals. Each of those girls knew God had called them to be Henry Jones' wife. I had never even heard him minister when I met him at a church meeting; however, my mother definitely knew who this gorgeous young man was. In fact, the Sunday that I finally agreed to accompany my parents to a conference meeting, I'm sure they had been praying that God would light a fire in our hearts for each other. You see, I had been going with a young man for three years and had always expected to marry him. He was from a great family who loved me, and I felt right at home with them. It did not matter to my mother. She knew that Henry Jones was the one and she would continually have my dad agreeing in prayer that God would answer their prayers.

THIS WOMAN LOVED HENRY JONES AS MUCH AS I DID.

When my boyfriend and I would have an argument, she would let me know that he was not the one. So, now you see why my mother was over the moon with excitement when Henry and I finally dated and then became engaged. Honestly, this woman loved Henry Jones as much as I did. She even let us kids know that he was her favorite child even when she was in her seventies. I'm sure it's because he became just like a true son to my parents and treated them with such honor. When my parents became unable to take care of their home, Henry was the one who suggested that they move into our home so we could be there for them. So, my dad lived with us nine years before he died, and my mom was with us fifteen years. Both of my parents never wavered in their love for my husband. Even when he was wrong in a decision, they would stand by his side because they believed in him. I could have never found another man who would have loved and served my parents any more than Henry did.

We knew, if doing good things for people could have altered the course of our lives, Henry would have been spared any hurts or diseases. However, that's not the way life rolls. As of today, Henry and one other cousin are the only cousins that have been affected by this horrendous disease. What is amazing is the preachers and musicians that are among the cousins in the Jones family. They are all very close and I still remember the last reunion when the cousins brought guitars and keyboards and spent the afternoon singing and playing. Honestly, the Joneses' extracurricular activities always involved church.

Henry's dad was the first to be diagnosed with Alzheimer's. We were in our twenties and busy starting a new church in West Point, MS. We had never been acquainted with anyone with a disease that could cause memory loss which would affect the entire family. Who could have known that Henry's dad would totally forget that Henry was his son? I remember our family traveling to Burlington, NC to visit him and his wife, Arthina. Arthina worked in a small sock factory and could bring Henry's dad to work with her because he had become unable to stay alone. We were totally shocked when his dad did not recognize our family nor even his son.

Henry was standing with his dad just loving on him when his dad told him that he had no money. He said his family needed food and he needed to borrow a few dollars. Henry pulled out some cash and gave it to him as he stuffed it in his pocket. Henry later told Arthina, his stepmother, that he had given his dad some money because he said he was broke. She let Henry know that he was never broke. She always kept a hundred-dollar bill folded in his wallet in case he needed it; however, he had no idea that he had a wallet besides the money. We were devastated that we would never again know the man who had been so alert, alive, and now was totally dependent on his wife to do everything for him.

I never thought that this scenario would play out in my home forty years later. I had no idea that this horrendous disease would change our family dynamic and steal the life out of the most vivacious man that I had ever met. And yet, I now am alone with just my family and my memories because the man, Henry Jones, has gone to his eternal home. Even when Aunt Mary Lee was moved to a nursing home because Uncle Leon could not provide the security and protection that she needed as a caregiver, Henry and I did not associate that this disease was running through his genes.

We never saw it coming

Eventually, Uncle Reuben began having problems with his memory. I remember one visit when we were just trying to make small talk with Uncle Reuben. One of his grandchildren came up behind him and was signaling to Henry that his granddad was crazy because he could not carry on a conversation. In fact, it made no sense at all. The little grandson meant nothing by it. It was the only way he could describe his granddad at that time. Yet, Henry left that day letting me know that situation had really affected him. After all he had done for the Kingdom of God, how could anyone disrespect Uncle Reuben? Of course, he later realized the whole scenario had affected him because it was just one more family member who was being taken down by this awful disease. Even after Aunt Mary Lee and Uncle Reuben passed away, we just kept living life as normal because that's what you do. You can never allow fear to rob you of your life.

Even families that have cancer or other devastating diseases that have been passed through generations, it's up to us to live life to its fullest. I remember when Henry went for a physical and completed a health background form, the doctor let him know that he really needed to consciously take care of himself because of the heart disease, diabetes and Alzheimer's in his family genes. He jokingly told the doctor how much he spent monthly on vitamins and herbs and gym memberships. He meant he would live healthy until he couldn't. That's just what he did.

In our twenties, we began taking vitamins and purchased our first life insurance. Henry Jones determined that he would take care of his family and would live a healthy life to be there for his family. It worked until it didn't. Really, we were as busy as possible traveling throughout the world ministering while mentoring pastors known as our spiritual sons and daughters.

Then, in 2005, we received a call from a spiritual son who was pastor of a church that had been planted out of our congregation in Jonesboro, GA (metro Atlanta). He was moving to another city and the church would need a pastor. It would be our responsibility to determine the direction of the congregation and church property. After much prayer, Henry and I determined that we would become the pastors in that season of our lives. We knew we could still travel in missions and grow the local congregation. So, we purchased a home in Fayetteville, GA and moved to our present location. Life was going as planned and we were enjoying the pastorate of this small congregation while we kept mentoring our pastors. How could life get any better?

Every storm runs out of rain!

five

It's Easy to be Angry and Hard to Understand

The Last 'I Love You'

While having lunch with one of my grandsons, he explained that he had to go through inner healing because he was becoming disconnected from God. How could a God who loved his Papa allow such a horrendous disease to affect the man who had given his entire life for the sake of the gospel? He explained that a speaker at a retreat that he had attended had given him the answer he needed to just stay connected as a child of God. The first time he ever heard God speak as he heard, "Your Papa's spirit is already with me. That's just his human home that is sick. I've got him."

Dementia is just one of so many diseases that afflicts the human body and can, in turn, cripple an entire family. I can tell you that, when the doctor gave us the diagnosis, I had no idea how to navigate the course nor could I have ever expected the nights of sleeplessness and weariness that would be a daily occurrence for weeks on end. Even though people could see that he was not his usual flamboyant self nor was he the self-assured pastor and leader of leaders during his last years, he would do a great job of covering up his inabilities. When asked what foods he would like to eat, he would immediately ask you what you were eating. If asked where he would like to go today, he would ask you the same question. He never responded as though he was lost even though we knew he was having a difficult time staying connected. This man who controlled every conversation began withdrawing into his world of silence.

Even though he was my constant companion for the first few years of his illness, he would be so excited that we were shopping or going to church. When we would be out shopping, I was always trying to cover him as he would reach out to babies and children lovingly. Of course, I was always afraid the parents would think he was a dirty old man, a pedophile or worse. So, I would immediately sweep in to save his reputation, I thought. I would let the parents know that we were grandparents of five grandsons and my husband had dementia. I think I realized during this transition of becoming his caregiver how controlling I had become.

Every Day was a New Day

Of course, every day was a new day. I did not understand the different stages of dementia until I would be thrown into a new situation, and then, I would remember what I had read. People that know me understand that I am always trying to get the details, to stay connected to the latest and greatest vitamins, herbs, medical breakthroughs, even though I totally walk by faith. I visited a dementia support group one day and decided I would rather not know than sit in a session with spouses telling each other how horrible their week had been. All I knew was that I would get through this and my husband would be with me in my home.

Rob, Kimberly and I even went to a seven-hour seminar one day with a neurologist and representatives from the Alzheimer's Association. In that meeting were at least eight husbands whose wives were already in memory care homes and were just trying to understand the disease that had taken away their spouses. This meeting was one of the most informative of all I had attended. There were no major breakthroughs in healing this disease, and no medicines that truly worked. This was what we were hearing. Each prescription was to try to maintain the loved ones' (LO) mental condition at that level; however, as of yet, no one can pinpoint the cause. That's the answer we always received when asking for help in making life bearable for the LO.

Every week would be entirely different. The day Henry slipped out of my house and was missing was a turning point for me. I had read this would happen but could not grasp the magnitude of fear that can hold you when you have no idea where to look for your loved one. And you know they cannot find their way home. Several times, our grandson, Morgan, would begin the search in his car, up and down the streets, looking for Papa. He would find him and bring him home. We knew this could eventually become disastrous, so our next move was to order locks for memory care patients to be installed on the tops of our doors to keep him inside.

One of his last escapades was the day the healthcare nurse visited to get our vitals and checkups for the insurance company. Henry was the first to be checked and did very well When it was my turn, I was getting my blood pressure checked when my daughter called me on the phone and asked if I knew where her dad was at that time. Of course, I knew. He had just been in the kitchen with us. She laughingly explained that he was sitting in her bedroom letting her know how much he disliked that lady that was at our house. He said, "I love Ann, but you know how she is. She lets anyone come into our house I didn't like that woman." He then began describing how big that woman was to him. Kimberly

I LOVE ANN, BUT YOU KNOW HOW SHE IS!

videoed him holding his hands out as far as possible and letting her know that woman was huge, and he definitely did not like her. I was so embarrassed because I had Kimberly on the speaker phone because the lady was getting my blood pressure. That sweet woman looked at me and said, "I thought we did really well together."

Then several days later as we patiently waited for the locks to arrive in the mail, I lost Henry again. I was shouting his name throughout the house but no answer. I then ran out into the yard and around the house. Then, my next move was down the street. As I crossed the street, it began raining and I saw a figure riding a bike in the rain. It was Henry. When he got home, he let me know that he couldn't find Kimberly's house. That was only a few days after he had run away, as he said. Now, Kimberly only lived about two blocks from me, but you needed to cross a four-lane street to get to her street.

You never knew when you would receive the last "I love you" or even "good night." As I have said, Henry did go with me everywhere. Grocery store, Lowe's, and Walmart. Rob and Kimberly had purchased a GPS watch so we could begin tracking Henry even if he became lost. One day, we were in Marshall's. Because he loved trying on shoes, he was sitting on a stool in the shoe department. I knew he would stay busy for a few minutes, so I went to the next department to check out jewelry. I kept looking in the shoe department to make sure I could see his white head. He always had the most striking hair so you could find him almost anywhere. Until that day. I didn't see his head. I went racing to the stool where he had been sitting and he was gone. I was running all over Marshall's because I did not know how to think as he was thinking. I looked at my iPhone app and it looked as though he was in the parking lot, so I race out of the store. I would look outside before I had the management alerted that a dementia patient was missing. This was the conversation screaming in my head as I searched frantically.

A New Pair of Shoes

Honestly, I think I tried to do it all myself because it was also embarrassing at first. My husband was Mr. Personality. When he walked into a room, everything changed. He was a pacesetter, a leader of leaders, and now it was as though I had an adult child by my side. On this day, I would have yelled it over a megaphone because I was becoming accustomed to the ups and downs of a disease that had slowly taken over our lives. I was in the parking lot screaming for Henry when I turned toward the store, and there was Henry walking out with the biggest smile in a new pair of shoes. How in the world could he have worn a new pair of shoes out of that store when they have sensors on everything? That was my thought process. I then escorted him back into the store to find his shoes which were not laying in the aisle. In fact, I had to search through boxes until I found the shoe box in which he had stored his shoes. He always was a clean freak and would be cleaning cabinets and even the bathroom sinks. So, I was not surprised that he had put those shoes in a box. I did not have to get the store managers involved that day; however, several days later my fears came to pass.

We were in Lowe's and Henry needed to use the restroom. I escorted him to the men's room and began looking through the aisle as I waited for him to come out. After several minutes, I was sure he had completed his task and finally, I knocked on the door. No answer. I then opened the door and called his name. No answer. He had left the restroom and walked down another aisle and I was frantic. I knew this store was too big for me to find him alone. I began running down the aisle to the front exit and, as I saw employees, I was describing my husband who was a white-headed man in a blue shirt with dementia. I had lost the feeling of being embarrassed and now fear had taken its place. What if I could not find him? What if he was alone all night somewhere? What if he was outside and hit by a car? The what ifs were screaming at me as I raced through the store. Then, I looked up and Henry was being escorted back into the store by an employee. Oh, Henry was happy as he could be to see me. He thought he had lost me, but I had lost him. I knew our times of going everywhere were coming to an end. I knew life as usual would never be as it was. I cannot tell you the many levels of sadness that overtakes you as you slowly lose your best friend, your husband, the love of your life.

Henry probably suffered from Vascular Dementia. Why 'probably'? Only an autopsy would have been definitive. Of course, his hospice nurse was the one who even tried to assume this was his condition. We had been visiting a neurologist for five years and, not once had he given us anything but 'early onset dementia'. I guess the early was because Henry was only sixty-seven years of age. This age sounds so young and yet, I am now acquainted with families whose loved ones have full-blown Alzheimer's at sixty years of age. Of course, our neurologist informed us that probably half the population in the next generation will be diagnosed with some form of dementia because they are not exercising their brains. He explained that, because our children and grandchildren use computers for everything, we no longer are stimulating what God has given us to use. This made so much sense to me. How many of you know anyone's phone numbers today? I know that I could not make it one day without my iPhone, iPad and computer.

Most people are more familiar with Alzheimer's disease today. Of course, so many people call it 'Old Timer's Disease', and they use that name for all dementias. However, there are so many more types. While Alzheimer's falls under the Dementia umbrella, there is something called mixed dementia. This means you could have more than one kind. According to the Alzheimer's Association, 50% to 70% of dementias are Alzheimer's, but there's also Lewy Body Dementia, Parkinson's Disease with Dementia, Creutzfeldt-Jacob Dementia, Normal Pressure

Hydrocephalus and Pick's Disease. I've heard people say that these illnesses are long goodbyes. However, I can tell you that watching your loved one lose his mind and body is one of the most horrendous challenges that can happen to a family. Our actual journey lasted five years, four months and three days after the initial diagnosis.

According to statistics, it is reported that there are five million people today afflicted with these memory diseases today and a new case of Alzheimer's is diagnosed every sixty-six seconds. You better believe that I faithfully take nutrients to feed my brain. When you realize that there are two principal types of the disease: early onset AZ or dementia which generally starts before fifty-years of age and late onset AZ or dementia which generally starts after sixty years of age, it just adds to your confusion. Are you in shock? Haven't you always thought that seniors should be in their late seventies or eighties when their memory seems to go? I think this is why I did not know where to go for help to understand what was happening to our family.

Really, I know that this disease did not just start with my sweet husband five years ago. Actually, he had a heart procedure four years prior to the initial diagnosis and had four stents placed in his heart vessels. So, that is really the reason they assumed it was Vascular Dementia. The neurologist said, "So goes the heart, so goes the brain." If the heart has clogged arteries and vessels, you just assume that the brain does also as it mirrors the heart. Have you ever heard this? I had never even thought about the end results of a heart procedure affecting the brain. I can tell you that, about eight or nine months after Henry's heart procedure, he was not the same vivacious, take-charge leader he had been our entire marriage. He began getting confused and, one day, even could not find his way home.

SO GOES THE HEART, SO GOES THE BRAIN!

I honestly did not think about memory loss. Somehow, miraculously, I was able to direct him home that day. I had no idea it was the beginning of the end. I thought it was side effects of heart medications. So, on our next follow-up visit to the cardiologist, I was full of questions. Why is my husband losing his thought process? Why is he getting so forgetful? Check out his medications. Of course, the cardiologist assured me that his medications were not causing him to forget. This went on for two years.

He was still preaching, pastoring, traveling; however, I was behind the scenes preparing sermons and prompting him before he spoke. I'm sure many people thought I was one more controlling wife, but all I was trying to do was protect my husband. I would anxiously explain to his primary care doctor that something was wrong; however, I could not get an answer. Until that fateful day when Henry's appointment was scheduled while I was meeting with a church member. So, I arrived thirty minutes later. His doctor immediately informed me that he was sending him to a neurologist. He had not realized how much Henry depended on me to answer all his questions until I wasn't there.

Honestly, there was no one in my world who could give me reasons why we were traveling down this path of life. It's easy to get so frustrated with the medical community because you wonder why, after all these years, they still do not have an answer to the why. When Henry's dad passed forty years prior, we just accepted that no one understood this disease. However, forty years later, I wonder why in the world the billions of dollars that are going into research have not pinpointed any reason why these diseases are still spoken about in terms of millions. I can tell you that each person afflicted is someone's loved one. These diseases are still heartless to the victim and caregiver alike. Dementia brutalized Henry and stole the love of my life from me. It altered him, us and me.

I determined that we needed to see a family estate attorney to assist us in navigating our journey so we were accompanied by our son, Rob, to get the much needed information. Honestly, it was well worth the money spent to get the directions in moving bank accounts, getting a quit claim deed so the mortgage would be changed from Henry's name to my name, making sure the will was correct in case Henry would ever need long-term care in a nursing facility. I am so thankful that, because we were facing the most horrendous challenge of our lives, we did not worry financially. Every step of our financial journey had been taken care of so at least that was one less worry for me.

I am on my feet today living life confidently because Henry taught me to walk by faith. We never allowed life challenges to steal our focus, so I got up the day after he died and started living life as normal as possible. I refuse to allow a disease that has touched millions of lives to steal my joy. I refuse to allow brokenness and aloneness to steal my focus. I am beautifully and wonderfully made by God and realize that, when Henry went to his eternal home, God assured me that He would be my husband.

Give the bones to
Henry Jones.

six

Meet the Joneses

Just Ordinary People

We had started our marriage in a little white church, which was pastored by my dad, on a Sunday afternoon and immediately stepped into the flow of evangelism that Henry had started at the age of sixteen. This girl, who had only traveled to Florida with her parents to visit relatives, transferred her closet into his automobile and began a journey into her future while staying in the homes of pastors the first year of her marriage.

The last weekend at home with my family was so unsettling for me that I had to struggle to find that excitement that most girls experience when they are preparing to walk down the aisle to say "yes" to the man of their dreams. The month was March, and yet, so much had already taken place the first three months of the year. My mom was involved in a catastrophic one-car accident during the Christmas holidays while my family was visiting their extended family two hundred miles away. I had stayed at home because of work and planning wedding activities. About midday the day after Christmas, I received an urgent call that my mom was in the emergency room of the local hospital and I would need to leave immediately to be support for my dad, brother and sister. When I arrived, I was shocked to see my mom, unresponsive with dried blood all over her face and body. She needed to be cleaned up as the hospital staff was unsure if she would make it through the night.

This was one more time that I urgently prayed that God would give us a miracle. Our little family had been through more crises than anyone I knew. I was ready for a breakthrough. I reasoned with God that we had lost my brother, Randy, and I could not imagine losing my sweet mom. She had been fighting for sanity and peace of mind most of my life. I could not even think beyond our circumstances as my fiancée, Henry, was by my side. What if Mom didn't make it? What if it would be just Dad and us kids? How in the world could I leave my little family and evangelize with so much heartache at home? This was my world. I struggled to figure life out day by day as Mom miraculously made it through the night and then the week. Our holidays that had begun so beautifully had turned into a nightmare that lasted longer than the night.

When Mom was released from the hospital, she was transported two hundred miles to our house in an ambulance. Her arm, leg and foot were broken, and she had several pins in her joints. She would be bed-bound and in a wheelchair for months. I was working until I got married, but how in the world could I get married and leave my family in that condition? I asked myself this question many times throughout each day. Yet, my parents continually encouraged me to keep planning the wedding. We had no idea that Mom would need several more surgeries throughout the year.

We knew it would be a small wedding. My mom was unable to do anything except be pushed down the aisle in her wheelchair. So, I planned everything. Even purchased my dress, went to the fitting, purchased flowers, even the reception. Honestly, the entire three months was surreal. Today, it is as if I was in a dream and was waiting to wake up.

That Sunday afternoon when I became Mrs. Henry R. Jones Jr., I felt as though I had aged ten years in three months. Anxiously waiting to see if Mom would be able to attend the ceremony, trying to figure the process of Dad caring for the entire family while pastoring, and figuring my own personal life out was a fulltime job. I knew when I married Henry that he would pack my clothes in his car, and we would leave for weeks or months at a time. As I rehearse that time now, I realize that God was already showing me how to walk by faith. I had no idea what our life would look like. We would be staying in the homes of pastors and preaching to new congregations while struggling to get to know each other.

You see, we really did not have any normal dating rituals as most couples. Henry would be gone for several weeks, then drive in on a Saturday to leave on Sunday for the next revival. The only way we got to know each other was in letters. We wrote a letter a day to each other. Do you believe I still have a bag of love letters that spread over months of our courtship and yet, we were together maybe ten times in five months? Then we usually were going to church where he would be preaching. I remember riding home with him from a church service when we were listening to gospel music on the radio. He started singing along and I assisted, except it wasn't

IT WAS AS IF I WERE IN A DREAM AND WAITING TO WAKE UP.

pleasing to the ear. So, we stopped singing and he prayed that we would fit together in life and in ministry as God would have it. Funny thing is, after that prayer, we began singing together and it just worked. In every revival, we always sang, me on the organ and him with his cobalt blue electric guitar with the Fender Rhodes amp that was almost as tall as he was.

I still am amazed how in the world we carried so much in our automobile. Our entire closet and musical instruments filled every inch of space. We finally decided it was time to look for a home on the road, a travel trailer. Our first trailer was only seventeen feet long, a little over three times longer than me. It was so small that we would fold up our table to make our bed. We would sit on the potty to use the shower, and, of course, only one at a time in the bathroom. Honestly, when I realized I was pregnant, I had no idea where we would store a baby and all his paraphernalia.

It was Such an Exciting Time to Be Alive

Do you know I still remember when the Apollo 8 with the first humans onboard was launched? Henry and I were doing the front work, leading singing and playing the music, for a tent revivalist. Immediately after we finished singing, we were behind the platform with the small television showing the Apollo launch. It was such an exciting time to be alive, we thought! It also was the week of my first birthday after marriage, and my brand-new hubby forgot. Oh, I was a hot mess. I waited all day for anything to happen, but it didn't. Finally, about 9 PM, I started crying. How in the world could he forget my birthday? Poor guy! He had never had to jump through so many hoops for any girl, and now he was married to an emotional wreck.

I think one of the most memorable moments of my life took place immediately after this tent revival. It was about 7 am, and I was driving our car and pulling our trailer to our next revival meeting. Henry was sitting beside me while reading his Bible. Suddenly, he began crying profusely and fell in the front floorboard. Listen, I had no idea what was happening. Finally, when he could talk, he looked up at me and said that God had just given Him a revelation of God in Christ, how powerful was the name of Jesus Christ. How God had truly sent his Son to earth by robing Himself in flesh and becoming human to show us how to live for

Him. He let me know that he was going to preach what God had given him if he lost his family, my family and even me. This statement was made because he knew he would be a radical for Jesus Christ, unlike anything his family had been.

It totally shook me to my core. I had never seen him so passionate, and yet he had been spending most nights in the Bible. He was so excited about the revelation knowledge that he was receiving that he would try to wake me up at 3 a.m. to show me what he had found. Hey, one thing you don't do when I get to sleep, especially when six months pregnant, that is to attempt to wake me up to read to me. What in the world was he thinking?

About six weeks later, we had purchased our own tent, chairs, organ, and truck and was in a revival meeting in his hometown. During that time, we both were re-baptized as adults. We both had been baptized several times as children because our fathers were pastors and were continually baptizing the members. It was a landmark decision as we were baptized together and allowed the name of Jesus to be applied to our lives.

There Have Been So Many Firsts

There have been so many firsts in our lives. I look back at the Henry Jones who was always a leader of leaders. When he made a decision, we all knew it would be carried out. Even my parents, who loved him just like a son, would have followed him to the ends of the earth. So, after six years of evangelism, we decided it was time to settle down since we had two children who would be starting kindergarten.

By the way, I guess I should tell you a little about our days in the travel trailer with two kids and no dog. No, we certainly did not have room for even a dog. Do you believe that I even carried my sewing machine and worked feverishly during the day sewing clothes for the munchkins and me? I became experienced at even sewing Rob's little suits and ties.

Of course, Kimberly had everything matching, even her little lacey panties. Thank God they did have twin beds in their own room, and we used the couch up front which was a comfortable bed. Our entire family adjusted so well to traveling and just made it work. We were in church six nights a week with Mondays for rest or traveling. I would take the kids and do laundry at the local laundry mat weekly. Honestly, there were times that I would get concerned because my little girl would try to go to any stranger that walked into the laundry mat. I was continually holding her or trying to keep her corralled. Who could have known that, as an adult, this little girl would reach the masses for Jesus Christ?

Our family began just as our marriage did – little money and lots of love. When Rob was born, Henry had a JCPenney credit card, so he traveled fifty miles to another town to buy clothes for our little baby to wear home from the hospital. You know what? We really did not realize we were poor or with only a little. We were young, with vision, and knew we would make it. Then, two years and eight months later, Kimberly came early. We had been in Miami, FL in revival and knew we had four weeks before Kimberly was due to arrive. I had seen a different doctor each month in different states, and the doctor in Miami instructed me to lay in the back seat, take breaks every hundred miles and take it easy. I could do that, I thought. Then, when we arrived in Greensboro, NC, Henry took a flight out for Denver, CO to preach a revival. I drove our car and trailer two hundred miles to my parent's home.

Who would have known that this little jaunt would trigger Kimberly's arrival? Two days after arriving at my parents' home, I was awakened suddenly and knew it was time. I woke my mom and drove her to the hospital, locked the car and checked myself in. Can you see a pattern here? I was becoming a controller. If I wasn't in the driver's seat, I wasn't sure it would happen. Eight hours later, I was introduced to this vivacious little five-pound two-ounce bundle who had refused to be born normally so she arrived butt-first with her leg wrapped around her neck. Who could have known that forty-eight years later, Kimberly, who was almost named Tabatha, is this colorful bundle of joy who spends her time loving people back to life. So, the proud daddy arrived from Denver nine hours after her birth and walked into our hospital room with flowers and candy. I had my hair curled and thought I looked gorgeous with my adorable baby girl fully dressed. Now listen, it was 9 p.m. and I had just had a baby that day however, I wanted that first meeting of father and daughter to be the most memorable experience that Henry had ever had. It worked because his family meant everything to him. This trip to Denver was one of his shortest revivals of that time. What was supposed to be two weeks was two days. So, two days after Kimberly was born, Henry flew back to continue his revival. On the way home from the hospital with my dad, loneliness enveloped me. I knew why Henry had to return to continue the revival, but it did not make me feel any better. Thank God for my parents who stepped in and assisted in helping when needed.

This immature girl who had just delivered her second child and had thought she could not face life unassisted was learning to stand up and face tomorrow knowing that you don't worry about tomorrow because today has enough worries of its own. I had read this verse in Philippians chapter four many times so, in this season, I was learning to stand on God's Word for survival. Paul, the apostle, told us to not worry about anything but to pray about everything and tell God what you need. Then His peace will envelope your heart and mind through Christ Jesus our Lord.

> *6 Don't worry about anything; instead, pray about every-thing. Tell God what you need and thank him for all he has done. 7 Then you will experience God's peace, which exceeds anything we can understand. His peace will guard your hearts and minds as you live in Christ Jesus.* Philippians 4:6-7

Faith doesn't allow
life challenges to
control us.

seven

Miracles, Signs & Wonders

It's a Faith Walk

*T*his man that I married totally walked by faith. He would speak a word and then walk it out until it happened. We did not speak doubt. We knew God was our source and we were demonstrations of that faith. We can truly say, after 52 years of ministry together, that God NEVER let us down. He saw us through the worst of times and the best of times. When we needed money for tires, miraculously we received enough for our week's sustenance and the tires.

Pastors called us in to "clean out their altars" as people would be seeking service after service for the Holy Spirit. Henry became known as the evangelist who would not hesitate to pray for anyone and everyone to be delivered, and they were. I remember one camp meeting in Louisiana. After church, Henry, my sister, Pamela, Rob, Kimberly and I went to a restaurant to eat. There was a table full of pastors who always hung out together. They were the ones with, in those days, the big churches. We call those churches now 'Mega Churches'. Of course, their churches were not five or ten thousand, and yet, they were great churches that all the evangelists enjoyed in ministry.

When we walked in, the pastors began joking with my husband, the evangelist. He had a reputation of being radical and sometimes overboard with his worship. Sometimes it was outlandish and not what these prudish pastors were used to seeing. So, they were joking at the way he worshipped. One of the pastors made a comment that he would pull him up by the seat of his pants and sit him down. This very pastor was the pastor of the congregation where we would be starting on Sunday five hundred miles away. He would fly home and we would pull our trailer to his city.

He Did Not Retaliate

When we began our drive home that night, Henry pulled the car over to the side of the street, put his head on his hands on the steering wheel and wept. These pastors had embarrassed him in front of his family; however, he did not retaliate. When we arrived at our travel trailer, he assisted me in getting everybody ready for bed, then excused himself, went into the little bathroom with a pillow and sobbed. Listening to my husband crying uncontrollably that night awoke a passion in me to hear the voice of God. If he could show the love of Jesus to these haughty pastors who were trying to embarrass him, why in the world could I not do the same. These pastors were his mentors. We knew that our very livelihood was connected to them and God, of course. When he finally came to bed, I begged him to cancel the revival. We had churches waiting for us to call and say that we were coming. We did not need that revival. We had never called one pastor and asked for a service. God always provided. Henry would not retaliate. He let me know that Jesus would be at that revival and so would we.

When we arrived in the city on Saturday, the pastor intentionally pulled us aside and instructed us to do whatever was necessary to bring revival to his church. Of course, we had a move of the Spirit unlike anything they had ever seen in that church. Today, there are men pastoring churches who were part of the harvest of that revival. Four weeks later, when we were leaving, the pastor handed us a special financial offering besides the honorarium. He let us know it was because he saw the love of Christ in us. Honestly, we never left a church without seeing revival, and most of our revivals were from four to ten weeks. We would pull our trailer onto the church property, hook up and expect to stay a while.

One pastor summarized our lives by saying that we were successful everywhere we went because we had to be. We did not have parents calling friends to get us a place to preach. If we did not have a move of God, we would not have a place to go next. I can tell you that, when we finally settled in West Point, MS to begin our first church, we had pastors calling us and letting us know that we were missing the will of God. The pastors that had scheduled us for future revivals were telling us that God would not have wanted us to settle down when we were so successful on the revival circuit. Yet, when we pulled our Airstream (by the way, we had finally arrived and purchased a thirty-one-foot trailer), into West Point, MS on that cloudy afternoon in January 1974, we told God it would be up to Him. He would let us know if this was our place. We would start with a revival and just see if it worked.

Guess what? It worked. Immediately, we began seeing people being changed and we knew God was in the middle of this move. Can you believe, forty-six years later, we still have friends that are just like family to us from West Point who were part of that little congregation that we called First Pentecostal Church of West Point. The reason we ended up in a small town of ten thousand people is because we were preaching a youth camp in Noxapater, MS. We were scheduled to be there five nights and it ended up turning into a revival out in the country. People were driving in from everywhere. I think the one experience that turned the course for the youth camp to become a revival was the night Henry walked by a lady whose hand was crippled from a fall. He touched her hand as he went by praying. Out of his peripheral vision, he saw her hand snap back into place. It was a miracle! Everybody began screaming and shouting as she jumped for joy. This woman was pastor of a small group in West Point.

Beginning a New Life

When we ended the revival and left for Texas, we were pleasantly surprised when this pastor and a lady from her congregation showed up in the next church revival. They let us know that God had said that we were supposed to be in Mississippi. Now listen! Out of all the states, we had never thought of Mississippi as home. Now on this January afternoon, we are driving into this beautiful little southern town checking it out to see if God wanted us there. I'm telling you that we have always walked by faith, so why wouldn't we drive into this little town by faith. The weird thing is our automobile engine blew up on us as we entered the city limits. We had this beautiful Buick with this gorgeous silver Airstream, and we are stranded by the side of the road and only knew a hand full of people. Thank God, there was someone in that congregation who could repair our car. This man's name was James Paul Winter. Do you believe that, if I needed JP (as we called him) today, he would be on his way to Atlanta? I'm telling you that God always came through for us.

So, the people kept coming over the next months. In fact, the church would only hold fifty people packed into the pews, so Henry knew we would need to purchase property. We also needed a Hammond C-3 organ because we didn't think you could have church without an organ. So, two new purchases – land and organ. Then Henry started cutting trees on the church property so people could park around the church, and he changed the light bulbs in the church to a higher wattage.

Crazy thing is that some of the people did not like change. I still am amazed at this because, if you know us or our children, we are not the norm. Don't want to be. Henry also preached a sermon about scrambled eggs. He said that if you had been previously married, divorced and re-married and now were accepting Jesus Christ as Lord, you can't unscramble scrambled eggs. Just start your new life at the altar.

So, after we arrived home from youth camp in June, we were met by two of the deacons with a list of names of people who wanted us to leave. They didn't like the scrambled egg doctrine. Funny thing is the people whose names were listed had never even been to church since we had been pastoring. It was a Saturday afternoon. We had church scheduled for the next morning. I fell on the couch and cried and cried and cried. How in the world could they not love us when we loved them so much that we had sold our trailer, rented a house and now were planted for good in a place that didn't want us? That was the conversation going on in my mind until Henry Jones jerked me back to reality.

He let me know that the people may have asked us to come to West Point, but God was one who had sent us. If God sent us, people would not move us. So, Sunday morning, we go to church and he prepares to preach. He announces that there would be a church meeting on Monday evening. He let everyone know that he would be recording the entire session and he did. The place was packed with onlookers and members. As the meeting started, Henry announced that we would be starting a new church, First Pentecostal Church of West Point, in the American Legion Hall on Wednesday evening. We would be responsible for the financial portion on the organ, and those left at the church would take the responsibility of the land. There was shock and awe. "You mean you are staying in this town? Why?" My husband let them know that God had sent us to plant a church and it would be planted. He refused to ever allow the enemy to rob him of his purpose. He

GOD WAS THE ONE WHO HAD SENT US

67

was a fighter, a warrior in the spirit, and would never back down when he knew he was right.

It worked for us. We eventually purchased property and built a beautiful new building in West Point. When we began receiving phone calls from Atlanta, GA that a church was needed, it was one of the hardest decisions we have ever made in our ministry and marriage. How could we leave a place that we loved so dearly and begin again in a concrete jungle? It took months for us to finally give in to the will of God and determine that we would move. Forty years later, I am amazed at how God showed up every time and, even today, we have people in our lives that are walking testimonies about how God was always there right on time.

You can't unscramble
scrambled eggs.

eight

You Were Equipped to Endure Hard Times

Get Up One More Time Than You Fall Down

If you had told me I would be authoring a book today about my different seasons of life, I would have been in shock and awe. You see, when my husband met me, I was a society editor and photographer at the local newspaper in my hometown. I always dressed the part and because we were located in the same city as the largest Marine Corps base in the world, I was kept very busy visiting the officers' clubs, officers' wives' gatherings, weddings, etc. You see, I had a press tag on my car and could follow any ambulance, police car, get into all the ball games and clubs. I really did think I was somebody special. I was one of those who loved their job. It sure did not pay much but who cared. I was living at home, had my car, wore gorgeous clothes which I would purchase on lay away each season. Had a boyfriend. In fact, had been going with him for three years and engaged a couple of times. We would have spats and I would give him back his ring. Doesn't this sound so mature?

Then I met the Henry Jones. Everything changed. I was used to buying what I wanted when I wanted it. Even though I was not raised in an affluential environment, I had learned to be frugal in some areas so I could shine in others. My parents were not destitute nor rich. We were definitely middle class, and it really helped that my dad was a master carpenter and cabinet builder. We lived in a nice brick home because my dad built it. He was an extremely hard worker and, when my mom was doing well, she was a highly successful salesperson. I was amazed when she became part of the Home Interior Company. I still have a houseful of silver that my mom won because she knew how to sell. And became a star. I think, watching my parents fight through adversity, sickness, disease, and keep their focus on things above, God and others, it created in me a drive to do my absolute best in everything that I attempt. Maybe that's why I am so competitive. I tell people I compete with myself. I can blame it on my mom who had such strict standards that I knew I must make the honor roll in school, but I know I have a drive within me to succeed.

Accustomed to Hard Times

I am sure much of why Henry and I could plant our lives in a new city and start a new successful church is because we were accustomed to challenging times growing up. Our parents did not have the money to buy whatever we wanted; however, we normally received what we needed. I remember Henry telling me about the time his 1956 Chevy blew its engine. He did not have the finances to get the motor replaced, so he asked his father if he would go with him to the finance company to borrow enough to pay for the repair. His father agreed with the condition that Henry borrow an extra fifty dollars to co-sign for the loan. Henry did and he did not think anything about it. I was in shock when he told me the story. My dad would never have asked me for money if he had helped me; however, I did pay rent as soon as I got a job. I also worked two jobs during high school and even paid for my graduation cap and gown, ring, and then gave my parents my graduation picture. We never took finances for granted. We knew we would work or not eat.

So, when we married, we knew that, if we did not stay busy evangelizing, we would get jobs. Amazing how God, in His mercy, always kept us busy. When we were in West Point, we did not have enough income the first year to support our family so Henry would purchase a car wholesale, drive it three months, sell it and then buy another one. He did so well in the resales that he decided he would start a car business. I was amazed and still am amazed that the man became successful selling cars. He even became such a competitor for the local Chevrolet dealership that they eventually offered him the job of Sales Manager. They assured him it would not interfere with his church. Before the first month was ended, he had sold so many used cars that he was moved up to General Manager of the dealership. We then had no worries. He drove a loaner from the dealership. What is amazing is that we did not live off the finances from the car dealership. Henry gave that money to the church so we could build a new building.

Every season of our lives was entirely new experiences, new ways to trust God, new circumstances to stand on faith. During our season in West Point, we had six young adults live in our home at different times. The reason I even mention this is that those young adults are still serving God today and are actively leading congregations throughout the U.S. I still try to figure how three young men, my two munchkins, and my husband and me could live in a three-bedroom home with a bath and one-half. How in the world did we make it work? I do not remember ever feeling cramped and crowded. Of course, I did not have to stay in the guys' room with bunkbeds and twins. The most amazing thing is the phone calls I still receive from those guys telling me how much they appreciate me cooking and cleaning and washing their dirty clothes.

HOW IN THE WORLD DID I JUGGLE MY WORLD?

When did I live? How in the world did I juggle my world, pastor a church, and take care of my own kids? I had to have great kids who just went along for the ride. I do remember Rob sleeping in Kim's room because his room was full of young men.

I remember one Christmas when Rob enthusiastically unwrapped the drum set which was on his Christmas wish list and immediately started banging on those drums. Then Kimberly unwrapped a table and chairs, so we could do the teatime together (my idea). The drumsticks kept mysteriously disappearing, and my little boy was always searching for those blasted sticks. In fact, the entire household would be upside down looking for those sticks.

Finally, we understood the big picture. Someone in our house was hiding the sticks because they could not tolerate the drumming day and night. I shall not reveal the culprit as I want to stay friends for a lifetime. However, Rob did become an excellent drummer. Then, on New Year's Eve, our adult children, as we called them then, bought fireworks so we could bring in the new year explosively. Of course, they needed something to prop up the fireworks so, out came Kimberly's tea table. When the excitement was over and the fireworks were finished, Kimberly's little table suffered a fiery demise. The top was so burned from the fireworks that we never did get to use that table for our afternoon tea.

Calamities were expected when you had a houseful of adults and two children. One afternoon, Rob was riding Kimberly on the handlebars of his bicycle. Of course, I did not know what was happening in the street. I was busy cooking and cleaning when I heard screaming. Rob had hit a bump and Kimberly was bounced up and then over those handlebars. The jolt had caused her to bite the inside of her mouth, so off to the doctor we went.

74

One More Calamity

One of the worst calamities for Kimberly (do you see a pattern here?) happened in the fellowship hall of our church. Several of our ladies were taking their shift babysitting children in our church day care. Yes, I had started a daycare to assist in the mortgage payment on our new building. So, we had local children from 7 am to 6 pm Monday through Friday. This business worked so well because we became acquainted with local families who were unchurched plus supplied weekly income for our building project. One afternoon, immediately after lunch before naptime, I was huddled with the children while reading a book. Kimberly was making her way from the kitchen area when she slipped on an exceedingly small metal figurine which belonged to one of the children and hit the corner of a chair. Listen, I went into panic mode. My baby, who was three years old, was pouring blood from her cheek.

I immediately grabbed her up and ran to my automobile while screaming for the ladies to call my husband. Remember, at that time, there were no cell phones. I was holding Kimberly in my lap while driving and pressing a cloth against her cheek. Thank God, we were only two miles from the doctor. However, there is a railroad track running through the small town, and, wouldn't you know it, there was a train coming through town. Of course, you know I am speeding down the railroad track while trying to beat that train at the next crossing. I had no idea that my husband was doing the same thing on the other side of town. I don't know why in the world I would always go straight to the doctor and never the emergency room, but I did beat that train and was at the doctor in just a few minutes. They were waiting for me as they ushered Kimberly to the back. As they removed the cloth, we realized there was a gash on my babies' cheek so, the doctor knew it would need stitches.

By then, Henry had arrived and gave the needed assurance to do whatever was necessary to save my little girl's face. Well, it only took four stitches, but they were on the cheek line so, as they began their

WE WERE ALWAYS SETTING BOUNDARIES

process, they would encourage Kimberly to close her eyes. Do you believe that kid never closed her eyes? She watched the needle as it came and went into her skin and never flinched. We were all amazed at her pain tolerance.

Who could have known that twelve years later she would be involved in a serious automobile accident that absolutely robbed her friend of her dreams? One Friday afternoon, Henry, Rob, and I were at home when we received a phone call that Kimberly had been in an accident two miles down the road. We reacted immediately and was at the scene of the accident within fifteen minutes. Kimberly had been transported by ambulance to a local hospital, but her friend had been air lifted to a hospital in the city. One man who was standing nearby informed us that Kimberly had been having a seizure while in the front seat of the automobile, and he had kept her safe during this occurrence. Everyone informed us that her friend was in serious condition, however we knew we had to get to our daughter.

I watched God that day turn everything around for Kimberly. When we arrived at the hospital, she was being checked out by the doctors and we were given a good report. No broken bones and she would be able to leave the hospital with us. Take it easy for a few days and come back for a checkup. However, her friend was in a coma and in intensive care for six weeks. When my husband would visit while praying fervently for a miracle, her mom would be praying with her beads.

Eventually this young lady was released from the hospital but would never again be the same bright, energetic student she had been. I cannot tell you why in the world this would happen on a Friday afternoon; however, I can tell you that we covered our children in prayer daily from the moment they were born until today. I can also tell you that Kimberly had been making some unhealthy life choices that we were asking

God for wisdom and direction to change. Kimberly's friend had been a strong leader and, for some reason, in this relationship, Kimberly was a follower. Her friend did not believe in God, and we were continually praying that God would work out this friendship for His glory. So, on that Friday afternoon, Kimberly had been instructed to come home immediately after school. Instead, she and her friend were headed to the mall when her friend pulled out in front of a van who had the right-of-way. Life changed as it was.

As her friend recouped from her serious accident, it was as though they had never been friends. Kimberly cried more days about this relationship because she had really cared for this young lady as a friend. It was as though their friendship had been erased from her friend's memory bank. They no longer talked on the phone, had shopping dates nor studied together. It was over. We were prayerfully watching as God assisted Kimberly in moving on.

This answer to prayer in her teens is why we were able to watch our daughter make other life choices that would send her into detours away from her life call, and we still trusted that God would cover her in spite of her choices. Kimberly eventually moved to Columbus, OH for one year and was blessed to be on the music team at World Harvest. During this time, she made life-long friends that, even though she left and was gone twenty-five years, we have watched God restore these relationships.

From one relationship to the next

She then entered a relationship and marriage which was highly frowned upon by her mentors. Kimberly was determined to make this marriage work. I remember one afternoon, as she sat on my bed while holding her newborn, Lyncoln, and weeping because her and her husband of three years had just had a public confrontation which resulted in our family being stranded in Atlanta during the Olympics.

I explained that she did not need to allow this type of behavior in her relationships. God had made her a special one-of-a-kind strong woman who did not need to bow to the pressure of abuse. I was adamant that she had to decide to change her relationship with her husband, so her boys would have a good example to follow. As she was weeping and praying, the phone rang. It all started over. The same apologies and it will never happen again. Just give me one chance. I know we can make it work this time. I listened as she decided that day that she would do whatever necessary to make this one work.

So, she entered her roller-coaster nightmare which lasted for sixteen years before she finally said it was enough. I know, many times, men and women stay in relationships much longer than is necessary for the sake of the children, the parents, the public, the church. I can tell you that, I may have been with my husband for fifty-two years, but he never was an abuser. He never cursed me or called me names. He never showed me disrespect in front of my children. So, I had a real problem watching my daughter be abused, and yet, she will tell you today, that she was part of that equation. She had become very hard-hearted and even bitter, yet she absolutely loved that man. She was devastated when the marriage eventually ended. However, she knew she needed to set an example for two young men who would eventually become husbands. Neither of her boys are married today; however, they are two of the kindest and most compassionate young men that I know.

Now listen, just because I have had outlandish stories about my daughter, don't think my son was a saint, even though most of the time I thought he was. Personally, I think Rob's sons today are exceptional examples of good men because their dad tried so many avenues in his teen years and determined he would make a change for himself. For some reason, the young men of our church youth group liked peach coolers. Now, my husband preached against any kind of alcohol because his family had been alcoholics, so we did not want our children dabbling in anything that could become addictive.

If praying alone would have done it, our kids would have been saints and never tasted of those things that we called worldly. However, there were times when our kids just yielded to temptations. Because it was our anniversary, Henry decided that we needed to get a hotel room in North Atlanta and spend two nights together. We would return to be in church on Sunday. Our little angels begged us to stay alone those two nights. You see, we always had someone from church stay with our kids if we were going to be away one or two nights. Henry felt we needed to show our kids that we trusted them, so they could prove to us that they could make adult decisions. Rob was eighteen and Kimberly was sixteen years of age at that time.

After we had checked into our hotel, gone out to dinner, and returned to our room, we called to check on our little angels. Whoever answered the phone had no idea who we were, and we did not know them. Music was blaring, and you could hear people laughing and hollering. We were both furious. How could they do this to us and break our trust? When Rob answered the phone, his dad explained life as it would be after that evening. Get everybody out of our house, clean up and know we are coming home. Of course, we returned the next day to two repentant sinners who were so sorry that they had fallen into this trap. Their sentiments did not move us. They both were grounded immediately. Rob's keys were taken and they both would be relying on us to chauffeur for a while. We had learned that the greatest punishment for a driver is to confiscate his keys.

THEIR SENTIMENTS DID NOT MOVE US.

A few months later, things had gotten back to normal. Both of our kids were out with church friends for the evening. When they returned, Henry and I were sitting in the family room as they both came in and sat down. I can only describe Rob as one of the happiest kids I had ever seen that evening. His dad asked him if he had a good evening. Of course, he was jubilant. This is so embarrassing to tell you; however, we were naiveté when it came to marijuana or any types of drugs. We had never tried any recreational drugs so could not smell the odor of marijuana. Friends later told us, because they had experienced drugs, they could walk into any room and know if someone had used marijuana. We never would have known if, two years later, Rob had not gone through a session of deliverance with his dad. In the session, Rob confessed to so many things that he had done that Henry was in shock.

When he returned home and I asked about the session, Henry instructed me to sit down because I would be shocked. The most amazing result of that session was that Rob totally changed his life and began pursuing bible school and full-time ministry.

Nine months prior to this session, we had been vacationing with our two in Key West, FL the week after Christmas. On the night of New Year's Eve, our children wanted to attend a party in the resort with some kids they had met. "Yes, Mom, the parents will definitely be there. Yes Mom, we will return before midnight so we can pray the old year old out and the new year in with you and Dad." This was our conversation before the kids walked out.

At 11:55 pm, Kimberly and another girl burst through our condo door crying. When asked her brother's location, she blurted out that he was drunk and the other kids had wanted to drag him out to the golf course, leave him and tell us that they had no idea where he had gone. As we ran to the next building, we are both in our heads wondering where we went wrong. Why in the world would our kids feel the necessity to follow everyone in life and not become leaders in their own right?

When we entered that condo at 12:10 am, New Year's Eve, the place deserted, dishes piled everywhere, and our son was laying out in the floor unconscious wearing only a pair of shorts, my heart was racing with fear. Henry immediately reached down to pick up Rob while Rob began fighting his dad and yelling, "Put me down Dude." I was so furious that he would ever talk to his dad in that voice, so I am telling him off while Henry is letting me know that Rob doesn't know what he's doing.

PUT ME DOWN DUDE!

Miraculously, the young security guard appeared and helped Henry carry Rob back to our condo. They lay him on our bed as the security guard left. We hear from Kimberly later that this young man was the reason our son was drunk that evening. He had been daring anyone to face off with him in a drinking match of Vodka. What in the world made our son think he could handle a quart of Vodka still amazes me today?

Henry bathed Rob, changed his clothes and then lay down beside him through the night while watching over him to make sure he did not get sick. Kimberly and I were huddled together on the couch while we cried and wondered how did we end up here? We did not see this coming.

The next day, about 9 a.m., Rob opened his eyes and looked into the eyes of his dad. He immediately closed his eyes and turned his head. His dad asked him if his head hurt, and Rob replied, "No sir, but my heart does." He remained in bed the entire New Year's Day recuperating from the previous evening, and we returned home the following day. Riding up Interstate 75 toward home, it looked like a moving sidewalk. Everyone was sitting still for hours. It gave our little family time to just determine the why and how we were at this junction. Rob apologized, and he let his dad know he would step down from the drums because he was not qualified to be playing in church.

Henry immediately stopped him and assured him that, absolutely, he would be on the platform on Sunday playing because he needed to fight through this challenge. The enemy may have won this skirmish, but he hasn't won the war. So, that Sunday, Rob began his journey of figuring life out after the fall. I'm not telling you that he never fell again,

I'm telling you that he got up one more time than he fell down. What a victor! So, nine months later, he made the choices that determined his next step. Within four months, he became assistant to the worship leader at World Harvest Church, Columbus, OH, and then returned to us one year later to become associate pastor and then eventually senior pastor. Who could have known that he would use his experiences to become an amazing husband, father and pastor?

Trying to Decide Future

We also had one of those experiences with Kimberly after she returned home with her two sons in tow. Just because she had left her abusive marriage and returned to our house did not mean everything was working out for our daughter. Through the years, she had made so many errors in judgment that she was now, at thirty-six years of age with two boys, trying to figure the direction she should take for her future. She would get so discouraged because, at one time, she had been a prosperous business owner with a gorgeous home driving a Mercedes convertible and now she was living in her parents' upstairs bedroom with all of her earthly belongings in a storage unit.

When she moved in with us, Henry had laid out a plan. She could live with us as we assisted her with her boys however, we needed help in our church with worship. She was an awesome worship leader and singer, so it was understood. No compromises!

One Saturday after she had left work, she did not come home. The first three years, Kimberly was fighting her demons and, many times, they won. So, this night was no different. After midnight, we could hear her stumbling upstairs as she knocked the entire wall of pictures down. I was livid because her little boy of eleven was laying in my bed weeping because he knew she had been drinking. Henry made his way upstairs and quietly entered her room.

She was laying in the darkness and was barely making a sound. Her testimony is that she knew someone was there but did not want to face them. Finally, her dad spoke, "Kimberly, you may have a hangover in the morning, but you will lead worship at church because you are going to fight your way through this battle." She immediately opened her eyes and exclaimed that there was no way she could lead in the morning. However, that Sunday morning she knew her dad would not allow her to stay home and lose this battle. She did have the effects of her night of drinking, but she did pursue and win that battle. She says that, when her dad spoke in his non-judgmental voice to her that evening, she knew she was looking into the eyes of grace. She had never understood the grace that Jesus Christ had given us when He went to the cross for our every sin. He even said that it was finished. He covered everything that we would ever do. It's now up to us to repent and take a new step. This picture of grace in her father caused our Kimberly to determine that her life would be different. I still thank God daily for giving us the wisdom to be there when our two children needed to hear direction.

If God sent us,
people will not
move us.

nine

This Too Shall Pass

Storms Do Run Out of Rain

*T*here were certain times in our marriage that I could move into a world of comparison while looking at other young ministry couples who were blessed to have parents assist in finances and referrals for ministry. Our families were in ministry but always pastored small churches and lived frugally. They were not known throughout the Pentecostal church world outside of our local area. All they knew was beginning churches with Bible studies in communities and winning the lost for Jesus Christ. People would then donate land and the entire community would assist in raising a church.

So, we were not accustomed to the business end of ministry. Our families taught us to trust God in everything, and that's how we had been doing it. I've already explained that Henry only had one card when we married, the JC Penney card. I had none. I had always paid cash for everything except my 1963 Volkswagen Beetle which I had purchased immediately after graduation. Our only possessions had been wedding gifts and our travel trailer which was our home on the road. We didn't worry about household furnishings because everything we needed was self-contained.

So, this was the way we traveled until one day we passed an Airstream dealership on one of our ministry trips just to browse. When we left that dealership that day, we had not only purchased a new Airstream but also applied for a Master Card through the same bank that had financed our new home. The owner of the Airstream dealership was on the board of the local bank, so this man whom we thought was Jesus in skin, not only assisted us in financing our new home but also helped us obtain the credit card. He said we needed a credit card if we were traveling full time in ministry especially with our two-year old toddler and a new baby on the way. It was as though God had totally set us up for favor that day. We felt like adults as we signed the dotted lines to become proud new owners of the Mercedes of RVs.

It seemed as though we continually traveled from one life struggle to the next, and yet we made it. We rode down the interstate listening to gospel singing while singing along, "God's big tears are falling, and I know they are just for me. Sometimes the load gets so heavy, and His face I can hardly see. But every time I see a big tear drop, I forget all about my fears. You can call it rain if you want to, but it looks like God's big tears." We were always learning new songs because we were expected to sing before Henry preached each night.

After Kimberly was born, we realized it was much easier traveling at night with our babies so, immediately after church on Sunday night, we would load musical instruments, and Henry would hook up our travel trailer. We would be on the road again. We drove in two-hour increments through the night going from state to state while stopping to change drivers. We traveled thirty states during our first years of marriage and really loved doing what we did.

In fact, I remember one day traveling through Arkansas. Of course, there was no GPS at that time, so we had road maps and Good Sam camping booklets giving us information on RV parks along the way. We had notated an exceptional park, as the book had described, through the mountains of Arkansas, so decided that is where we would spend the night. The book described luscious grass, swimming, boating and picnic area. Sounded just like what we needed for a break from our reality.

As we pulled off the main highway and began our ascent up that mountain, I was already getting leery about our expedition. As we rounded the last curve and pulled up to a deserted park, we immediately knew we had to get out of there quickly. There was one disheveled man waiting for us to pull in, so Henry let him know politely that we definitely had made the wrong turn and would be on our way. We had our doors locked and it still was terrifying as we imagined what could have happened. I let my husband know that, if we were murdered, our parents would never have found us. Does this sound like the faith-filled couple who brought revival to people everywhere?

We knew This Too Shall Pass

We could never have dreamed that we would stay so busy in revivals that we only returned home to see parents one week in July and one week in December. It was the start of an amazing beginning doing full-time ministry for a fulltime God.

Any time crisis came, we knew this too shall pass. We knew it would be temporary. When people became unsettled in church as happens in most churches, we learned to go first to God for wisdom and then stand up and do what we did which was make decisions for the good of the church. I remember feeling crushed because a group of people were standing against us because they did not like the decisions that my husband had made. I could not figure how they would be against us when we loved them so much. My husband explained that we could not take everything personal that involved the church life. Because we were so consumed with ministry, we had a problem disconnecting our lives from the church life.

One of our most devastating times in our ministry was during the building of our new church in Atlanta. We had been in town four years, had exceeded all expectations, been the fastest growing Sunday School in our district and our Bible Quiz team had won the state quizzing tournament. We were riding high and saw no clouds on the horizon. One thing I've learned in this process of life. Life can throw you sucker punches. When you think things are going well, remember there are no promises in life except that Jesus will never leave you nor forsake you. He will be with you until the end.

A group of families decided they definitely did not like my husband's pastoring methods. After studying about insecure leaders, I can tell you that Henry Jones was not an insecure leader. Insecure leaders become the influenced rather than the influencers. A deacon who was leaving the church met with us to let us know that we were the best pastors he had ever experienced; however, he could not be part of the progressive church that my husband envisioned. We had a new building sitting on our property that was a testimony of faith; however, we needed the furnishings, the chandeliers, the carpet. Thousands of dollars were needed to finish the building and two hundred people eventually left, one family at a time. How in the world could we continue with church and keep the faith of the remaining families? That was my prayer every day.

Henry kept reassuring me that God would make a way. I knew what he was saying was true, but I needed God to do it quickly. One Sunday evening, we were having our usual service when two men stepped through the doors and stayed for the entire service. Immediately after church, one of the men found my husband and exclaimed that he had never heard of our congregation. He said he was passing by while on the way to another church in Atlanta when something told him to turn around and go back to the church he just passed. He did and he was overwhelmed with excitement. He also made a promise that he would have two pews filled the next Sunday because he had never heard such an amazing sermon as he had heard that evening.

We even purchased more land

Here is what God did for us. The next Sunday, the young man did fill two pews and then began filling pews every week until he had replaced every person that had left our church during that season. We were able to totally complete the sanctuary and move into the structure as had been planned. You see, when the deacon had announced to my husband months before that he was leaving, he had stated that the bank would own the building. How devastating was that? When someone you respect and love pronounces a curse on the very ministry that you have worked so hard to preserve. Of course, it did not happen. We have learned through experience that you do not have to receive those curses that people speak over you. In fact, we even purchased the land next door.

Henry and I had lived our lives so consumed by church and ministry that we had never been on a vacation with our children except to visit parents. When we finally took our first vacation, our children were twelve and fifteen years of age, and we absolutely did not know how to relax and understand that the church families would get along fine without us for a week. As a result of that weeklong holiday, we purchased a time share week which we would use annually so we could give our children normalcy. We used this timeshare week for over thirty years, and it did provide us with many memories that my family can now share with each other.

We walk by faith
and not by sight

ten

Mourn and Move

Just One Step at a Time

Because we left our homes at twenty years of age and became full-time evangelists, we truly were traveling nomads. I lost connection with family and friends in whom I had gone to school and those childhood friends whom I saw every day. It was as though we were totally writing our life story together, so we became accustomed to having a small group of friends. We had many acquaintances, but they were not the friends you called when you had problems.

So, in our twenty-sixth year of marriage, we hit a dangerous place personally where we could have said that it was over. We lost the flame of love and realized we had nothing in common but church and ministry. Our kids had grown up and married, and we were expecting our first grandchild. I came face to face with the insecurities that I had carried my entire life since my brother had passed. I had tried to love my family so deeply that I had tried to control everything about their lives. If I loved them enough, they would always love me. I think I was afraid of losing another love like my brother.

Even when my children were entering elementary school, I would dress them in bed, carry them to the kitchen to eat breakfast and then back to the bed for a few more minutes of sleep. Then I would transport them to school even though a school bus came by our house. There was no way I would have sent my kids on a bus. Even today, I wonder if that was out of fear, control or insecurity. I wanted to know everything going on in their lives.

So, when Kimberly was diagnosed with a learning disability, I thought I had failed. How could my child not learn when I would spend hours with her, if necessary, learning phonics? The problem was my child never understood phonics. It was like hitting a brick wall time and again and yet thinking the next time would not be as hard.

Life just kept moving as it does even with the challenges in school. Finally, Rob and Kimberly graduated and moved on. What does an insecure mother do when your kids no longer need you? Who would need me now? My husband certainly didn't need me to take care of him. He was a mover and shaker who controlled everyone's world. We had established a Bible college and was busy teaching days and nights. We would meet each other in passing, and when we were together, the conversation was always about church. It was as though we were standing on the edge of a precipice and losing our balance. The next move would send us reeling into the abyss of life. I will not go into the entire story of how we regained a love that had been dying, but I can tell you that we knew we were headed for separation or divorce. I had even instructed Henry to leave until he could figure himself out.

WE WERE STANDING ON THE EDGE OF A PRECIPICE AND LOSING OUR BALANCE.

One night about 3 am, Henry was away, and I was alone in my bedroom. I had Christian television on the screen and a gospel choir was singing soothing music as I was trying to relax for sleep. It wasn't happening. I fell on the floor, face down, weeping. I had come to the end of me. I could not keep living life as usual. With my face in the carpet, I took my hands and lifted them up to Jesus. I then prayed that He would take over my marriage and do what was necessary. I really wasn't praying for Henry. I just wanted peace. I had no idea what that would look like but knew I could not keep living life the way we were going. We were living in a house together, but we were not together. We were exhibiting to our church that everything was going well, yet our lives were falling apart, becoming disjointed at the seams. We had become great actors in this episode and now the curtain was going up, and everyone would know the end of the story. In fact, the week prior to this night, I had started packing my bag to leave, and Henry had knelt in front of me while holding me back. He was telling me that, if I left, he was going with me. How hilarious! He was the reason I was in this predicament. You see, where in the world could I have gone? My parents lived with us and I sure did not expect him to continue taking care of them alone.

It really was hilarious. We needed to become adults at forty-eight years of age, suck it up and do what was right. But what was right? My parents were still together after fifty years while his dad had been married four times and was still pastoring. We had a distorted view as to what our future would be. All I know is that, when Henry asked me to marry him, he let me know he wanted to live with me until death parted us. So where was this man that I had married twenty-six years before? That night, God honestly gave me a scripture to read from the book of Habakkuk.

²Then the LORD said to me, "Write my answer plainly on tablets, so that a runner can carry the correct message to others. ³This vision is for a future time. It describes the end, and it will be fulfilled. If it seems slow in coming, wait patiently, for it will surely take place. It will not be delayed. – Habakkuk 2:2-3

I was crying so hard that I could hardly contain my emotions. I grabbed a notebook and began writing a list of things I knew had to be changed for me to continue the life I was living. The first request was that God give me a husband who would love me as Christ loved the church as written in Ephesians 5.

25For husbands, this means love your wives, just as Christ loved the church. He gave up his life for her. 28In the same way, husbands ought to love their wives as they love their own bodies. For a man who loves his wife actually shows love for himself. 33So again I say, each man must love his wife as he loves himself, and the wife must respect her husband. – Ephesians 5:25, 28, 33

The strange thing about this request was that I did not write Henry's name in the request. I just knew I wanted a husband to love me as Christ loved the church and would lay his life down for me. I knew Henry loved people and gave his life daily for the church, but I did not feel that kind of love for me. I needed more than I was receiving in this marriage, and I'm sure Henry felt the same. Our problem was much larger than I can even speak about, but I knew God would have to work it out. We could not do it alone.

I wanted to tell you this story because I totally watched God perform a miracle in our marriage. I know it takes two people to make a marriage, but I had decided that our marriage may have been over at that time. However, God began working on both of us. It was a slow process while we still pastored our church and ran the Bible school. We deliberately determined that we needed time together, so we took a six-week sabbatical from pastoring and also went away for counseling.

It took us about three years of intentional building to recover what we had lost; however, we received much more back than we had given. The reason I tell this story is because, seven years later, Henry and I were moving to our present home and were packing up our offices. As

I riffled through my desk drawers and files, I found the notebook paper with the list of prayer requests that I had given to God seven years before. Also, one morning as I was standing in my kitchen during this time, my husband came in behind me, wrapped his arms around me and said, "Ann, I love you so much that I would take a bullet for you." Do you have any idea how I felt at that moment? I had asked God to give me a husband who would love me so much that he would lay his life down for me. I had never felt that in my marriage and now, Henry was answering my prayers.

I LOVE YOU SO MUCH I WOULD TAKE A BULLET FOR YOU

It's never too late. When you present your requests to God, you then just stand. I had lived a lifetime of trying to receive love by works, and now I realized that God would answer when you call. He gave me the husband I had always dreamed of but had no idea I could receive. The last twenty-six years of our marriage was the most amazing time of my life. So, daily I am thankful for every moment spent with the man of my dreams. That's why I am still on my feet, arising daily, thanking God for His blessings. Am I in mourning? There are times I get sappy with tears, but I remember the goodness of God and how He changed my marriage after I believed!

Ain't nothing to
it but to do it.

eleven

52 years, 3 months, 6 days

The Journey Has Just Begun

*T*he day I realized I could put a time frame on our marriage was an awakening for me. The one that had been my best friend, mentor, husband, lover and the father of our children was no longer in this realm. When Henry asked me to marry him, he had said he wanted it to last a lifetime. Of course, the bride and groom always walk down the aisle thinking this will last until death do us part. However, you really don't want to think about the death part. Yet, it truly happens. I am a living witness that I walk through the house that my husband picked out, lay down in the bed that he had to buy, sit down at the table that we argued about when purchasing because he wanted that very one, and I realize how much he had decided things would go his way. Oh, my goodness!

Now I must get up daily and think for myself. What happened to that strong-willed girl who had ruled her world until the flamboyant evangelist walked through the door? With all the ups and downs of life, I would not change a thing. We flowed from one process to the next as we traversed through this life together.

My parents were married fifty-four years before my dad passed, and I never dreamed they would live together longer than my vivacious hunk of determination. When Henry began getting more active in the late afternoons, Sundowner's they call it, I had no idea that he would stay up most of the night and then pass out on the loveseat in our bedroom. This man always slept with me even when we were upset. We might not be speaking but we were sleeping together. Then one night turned into every night.

THIS WAS ONE MORE ARGUMENT THAT I LOST

Finally, several months after sleeping on or folding up on the loveseat, he tried to get up on our bed to lay down. If it had not been so tragic, it would have been hilarious. You see, when we purchased our king-sized bedroom suite, I had argued that the bed was entirely too high. I wanted to be able to sit down on my bed, not climb up into it. Yet, this was just one more argument that I lost. Henry purchased his gorgeous bed, and now, he was unable to maneuver onto it. I looked at him one night when everything was going wrong and said, "Looks like the jokes on you Henry Jones. Now you can't even get up on your own bed that you insisted on buying." However, it wasn't a joke. I was so sad. I could not help him into the bed, so he just lay down on the loveseat.

When hospice came in ten months before he passed, the first order of the day was a hospital bed to be moved into our bedroom for Henry to be comfortable again. The sad part of this horrible disease called dementia is it comes in stages. As July and August turned into September, hospice had become a vital part of our family life. You see, before they were there, I was falling apart. How in the world could I keep this strong man who was determined to do things his way together? Yet, I knew there was no way I would ever move him into a memory care facility. I knew God would give me the wisdom to make right decisions. By this time, Henry could not hold a conversation with anyone; however, he still told me many times a day that he loved me.

By the sixth month before he died, Henry had forgotten his children's names. He would look at Kimberly as she assisted me in dressing him in the evening and say, "I love you Son." I began telling myself that, in case he forgot who I was, I wanted him to look at me and know the lady feeding and changing him really loved him. Because Henry was a people's leader, he was always so busy and, many times, our children did not get his undivided attention. So, now, in the seventh stage of dementia, Rob and Kimberly would sit beside their dad and hold his hand as they kissed on him. How does a 5'11" hunk of man become like a child and need to be bathed, clothed, fed and changed? That's the question we continually asked.

My Love Would Be Treated with Dignity

I made up my mind in the beginning that, no matter the price, the love of my life would be treated with dignity. Even when my children were encouraging me to return to aerobics, I was trying to plot the course. Everyone was letting me know that the caregiver must take care of themselves to be able to care for the patient. How could I leave for an hour in the mornings and make sure Henry was taken care of? Then Rob stepped in and began coming by three days weekly so I could slip out and take care of me. He would assist the nurse and CNA as they bathed and dressed Henry, then spend time with his dad until I returned. One morning Rob was sitting in the recliner as his dad lay on the bed. Rob had so many decisions that he was in the process of making and was thinking how much he needed his dad's input at this time. In a few minutes, Henry turned over, opened his eyes, looked at Rob and said, "It's not my decision to make, it's yours." Rob's eyes filled with tears as he realized his dad was telling him that whatever decision he made, it would be the right decision. Wow! Thank God that he had given our family peace as we navigated this difficult journey.

I now read posts from a Facebook group, Alzheimer's and Dementia Support Group, as family members are trying to figure out the course of action for their loved ones. No one can understand unless they have walked in our shoes the pain and suffering that accompanies every stage of this horrendous disease that steals mind and body of the most capable. Today, It's only been five months since Henry went to his eternal home, but it seems like just yesterday one moment and then a lifetime the next.

The last four months of his life, Henry was becoming immobile and could not walk without assistance. Because I am a health addict, I knew that if I had lemon water, a smoothie and oatmeal for breakfast, Henry would too. My kids always joked that he might not know us, however his body would always be healthy. The crazy fact is that his body was healthy with an unhealthy brain. Of course, we know that the brain controls everything about this body so, eventually it would shut down his system.

After he was bathed and clothed, we would move him by transport chair to the recliner in the living room so he could feel a part of the family. Even when the nurse wanted him to stay in bed, I rejected the idea because I did not want him to feel alone and insecure. I could not imagine the feelings he was dealing with as he tried to navigate life through feelings of insecurity and instability. I think the fear that would grip you knowing that you cannot figure life, people, and places out would be enough to cripple you besides dealing with the loss of feeding and clothing oneself.

HIS BODY WAS HEALTHY WITH AN UNHEALTHY BRAIN.

Because Henry had been a musician and singer, I kept worship music playing throughout our house to give him a sense of familiarity. I would sing along and try to get him to sing. I had seen other patients who could not carry on conversations but could sing familiar songs. Honestly, four months before Henry passed, he was walking through our house strumming his guitar. When he laid the guitar down for the last time and did not pick it up again, I realized what I was missing. He no longer would sit at the piano and play nor could he harmonize when I sang to him. Are you understanding the sadness that accompanies this sickness? You lose your loved one a piece at a time, a day at a time, then a moment at a time. Their body is there but that one that you talked to for hours at a time is nowhere to be found.

YOU LOSE YOUR LOVED ONE A PIECE AT A TIME

At first, you try to assist them in remembering those important things, the children, grandchildren, church, friends. Then you realize that this only makes their insecurity worse. When you look into their eyes, you see nothingness. They are not comprehending what you are saying, and yet, you keep trying just in case they might understand. Our prayer was always that he would receive a miraculous recovery. Kimberly faithfully spoke his miracle into existence. Her explanation was that we had allowed her entire social media community to be a part of our journey. So many of them are new believers who have been totally unchurched so, if they saw her dad receive a miraculous healing and his mind be restored, it would be the greatest testimony for the Kingdom of God. Sounded great, but we knew it was up to God to work that miracle. If He did, we would have been ecstatic, but if He did not choose to heal him on this earth, Henry would receive his total healing in Heaven. We refused to become angry at God that this man of God who we called husband, dad, granddad, pastor, apostle, prophet and friend had been chosen to live out this journey of dementia.

One week before Henry passed, we had no idea he would be leaving so soon. He developed a rash on his bottom which quickly turned into something serious, so he was immediately put on bedrest. After two days of using the normal ointments that were not working, we started soaking cloths in hot water filled with a cup of Epsom salt, then tea tree essential oil followed by corn starch. These old home remedies were working on the rash, so we were really encouraged on that Friday morning when Nancy, the nurse, and Tamika, the CNA arrived.

During his bath, Nancy realized that Henry was having a massive seizure that was affecting his brain. Prompted into action, she retrieved morphine and Ativan from our emergency kit in the refrigerator to counteract the seizure. She then informed us that Henry had started transitioning, and it could be up to eight days. We then called our family in to begin a vigil that would last until he was gone.

Four days later, Nancy was coming three to four times daily checking Henry's vitals as we hovered over him. It's so amazing how you can be watching your loved one go through the stages of dying and wonder how in the world people just keep living. Why doesn't the world stop until you can figure your present life out? Just because it doesn't. I'm sure it's the evolution process. People are dying as babies are being born. That Tuesday evening would be unlike any other day that I had ever witnessed.

Nancy left about 8:30 p.m. and let us know that she thought Henry would live through the night. Now two nights before this Tuesday evening, Kimberly and I were laying in my bed as Henry was laying on the hospital bed beside me. Because Kimberly has such a vast social media presence, she decided to go on Facebook Live for a few minutes and let her community of followers know our situation. She then asked me to pray. As I prayed, the Lord gave me a beautiful word about a transfer taking place that would involve gifts and anointings. So, I was expecting something spectacular the next few days.

I WAS EXPECTING SOMETHING SPECTACULAR!

About 10 p.m., my phone rang and our spiritual father and mentor, Bishop Bill Hamon, called to check on Henry and let me know that, no matter what happened, I would be strong and capable to face life. He then prayed that Henry would have a smooth and peaceful passing. Because the nurse had felt that Henry would not pass in the night, Rob and his family and our grandson, Lyncoln, had left for home. I hung up my phone, brushed my teeth and started to get into bed beside Kimberly. I turned to kiss my hubby good night and realized he was passing. I called for Kimberly, then phoned the nurse and the family to return immediately. I can only tell you what I saw.

Our family with the nurse was hovered over Henry's bed as we sang his favorite songs and praised Jesus for giving us such a good man to lead our family. The last words Henry heard were me telling him how honored I was to be able to serve him. When we all were standing in a world of silence, after Henry drew his last breath, Nancy asked, "What was that? I have witnessed hundreds passing, but I have ever experienced anything like this." We were able to explain that a soldier in the Kingdom of God had just stepped from this realm to the heavenly realm while being escorted by transport angels. Yes, I believe the angels had been in his room the entire week while waiting for him to release his spirit. What we all were feeling was an elevation taking place. Honestly, I have never experienced such glory in one setting.

He was a Seer to the Nations

In the book of II Kings chapter two, the account of the prophet, Elijah, being taken up in a chariot of fire reminds me of what we were experiencing that Tuesday evening at 10:47 p.m. When the Lord was about to take Elijah up to Heaven in a whirlwind, the prophet instructed his mentee or spiritual son, Elisha, to stay in Gilgal as he went to Bethel. Elisha let his mentor know he would not leave his side. Even as the prophets in Bethel were telling Elisha that Elijah was leaving, Elisha already knew it. Then Elijah travels onto Jericho then to the Jordan River, but Elisha was with him. He was determined he would be there when his leader was carried up in the whirlwind. When Elijah asked him in II Kings 2:9 what did he want Elijah to do for him, Elisha let him know he wanted a double portion of Elijah's anointing. He was promised that anointing if he was with his leader when he was taken up.

Our family had been promised a transfer of anointings, gifts and blessings when the patriarch of our family was caught up. We were determined to be in that room hovered over the bed as Henry Jones was caught up. Please do not misunderstand me. He was not Elijah, but he was called of God and had been called a 'seer to the nations.' He walked in a strong prophetic anointing with such wisdom that we knew it would be passed to his heirs. It's called legacy.

Elisha was there when Elijah was carried away in the chariot of fire. He did receive the double portion anointing and was able to perform twice as many miracles as his mentor. The Jones family is now walking into a new season together while knowing there were impartations on that evening of June 16, 2020.

The next Sunday, I was standing by my daughter, Kimberly, in church on a Sunday morning. We were all dancing and worshipping as she started dancing toward the altar, picked up a small piece of paper and danced back. Laid the paper on a table and a few minutes later, she rehearsed her steps. As she danced back, I said, "Okay, Henry, it looks better now." Her dad was known for his desire for excellence in the house of God. He would be re-arranging plants and picking up anything on the floor. Since he has gone to his eternal home, she has had walls removed and others painted and new flooring throughout our church. When you walk in, it looks excellent. My son, Rob, has taken on the responsibility of the patriarch of our family and is making decisions that, at one time, his dad would have made.

So, now we walk by faith and not by sight just like my husband taught us. I never saw him lose his faith nor his testimony. As long as he was in his right mind, he was praising the Lord and loving people back to life. We have pictures of him at the altar one year before he passed, when he was able to be in church. He had his arms around the congregants praying for them. It always made everyone weep when he would begin worshipping and dancing in church. Our entire family knows we were made for the battle. We are strong and shall endure until the end.

This too shall pass.

twelve

How in the World Do You Move On?

My Next Chapter

I still am amazed how I am sitting alone finishing a book that was started when we began our life together fifty-two years ago. No, I was not writing feverishly throughout the years because I was living life vicariously through our marriage while navigating the course of life. As I rehearse the how's and why's, I realize it totally did not take God by surprise when Henry succumbed to the complications of dementia.

I know, without a doubt, that God is at the helm of the Jones' ship. He has been navigating our course throughout history. So, you ask, how in the world have we managed to stay together when we could have chosen to separate, how have we been successful in pastoring churches even though it wasn't about the building, it was about the people, and how were we successful in seeing our children not only standing but still loving God and in ministry?

I'm so glad you asked because I can explain our process as we complete our journey of finishing the *Sleeping with a Stranger* book. Are you understanding the title now? You get the concept of why many days it seemed as though I was taking care of an adult toddler instead of caring for the man that I had loved all these years. It really did not matter his condition. I knew, without a doubt, that he loved me despite the illness.

There were so many favorite scriptures that I have memorized through the years that have kept my feet planted on solid ground. This sounds so anti-climactic; however, this girl had a problem memorizing scriptures. I have such an active mind that I would start reading and then see so many tasks that needed to be completed. So, my husband whom I called my walking concordance, would always guide me to the appropriate scriptures as I needed them. Then, one day I was reading Psalm 1 in the Bible. The first three verses captivated me as I realized there were blessings that were promised to us if we just allowed the Word to engulf us.

I kept reading the "Blessed are" scriptures every day because I realized that God had promised me blessings, but it was up to me to act out the scriptures. How would I become that blessed person if I did not know His promise? What is amazing is before the week was ending, I was quoting those first verses of Psalm 1 and realized I had my answer. Now I knew how my husband knew thousands of scriptures by memory. He continually read those passages until he had hidden them in his heart (mind).

¹Blessed is the man who walks not in the counsel of the ungodly, nor stands in the path of sinners, nor sits in the seat of the scornful; ²But his delight is in the law of the LORD, And in His law he [b]meditates day and night. ³He shall be like a tree planted by the [c]rivers of water, that brings forth its fruit in its season. Whose leaf also shall not wither; and whatever he does shall prosper. Psalm 1:1-3 (NKJV)

Are you understanding the simplicity of memorizing the Lord's promises? You will not receive anything from the Bible through osmosis. If it could have been, I would definitely have been the recipient. I would pray and ask God to please help me learn the scriptures. How could I speak to congregations for thirty years and not be able to quote scriptures? I think it's amazing how God will become what we need when we need Him. He knew I was ready to become a serious student of the Word. I ask Him daily in prayer to be Lord of my spirit, soul and body, heart, mind and will. This is a necessity for me because I am a strong-willed woman and try to regulate everyone's world around me.

I did not have any idea I was as I am until I came to the end of myself as the prodigal son did in Luke 15. This young man thought he was living life to the fullest after receiving his inheritance. Crazy thing is this young Jewish boy totally went through every penny of his money and was caring for pigs. How outlandish is that when Jews do not eat pork? He wasn't allowed to eat the pig's food, only care for them. He finally talked to himself, "Even the servants that work for my father have more than I do. Why do I not go home and tell my dad that I just want to be a servant? I do not expect anything else."

17"When he finally came to his senses, he said to himself, 'At home even the hired servants have food enough to spare, and here I am dying of hunger! 18I will go home to my father and say, "Father, I have sinned against both heaven and you, 19and I am no longer worthy of being called your son. Please take me on as a hired servant."' Luke 15:17-18

I was not in the pig pen of life when I came to myself, just going through the most troubling time of my marriage. I could not control my husband who was his own man. Today, we have an app on our iPhone called the Life 360 which allows our family to see where each member is located at any given time. I did not have the luxury of such an app twenty-six years ago, so I was always living in fear of what if. When I finally gave up and allowed God to be Lord of my life, the what ifs did not matter any longer. I could not control anyone when I could not even control my own emotions. What a great revelation!

That's when I found Proverbs 3:5-6 which let me know that I was to trust in the Lord with all my heart, don't try to understand my life situations but in all my ways, acknowledge Him and He would direct my path. I really pray that you can finish this journey with me with an understanding that life is a process. I did not become this strong woman who has become a widow yet walks in so much peace that my sleep last evening was so comforting by just living daily. It was much deeper and complicated than that. Even this morning as I write, I am taking one step at a time which is allowing the Lord to be all authority in my life.

Every day I let myself and everyone around know that my weapons are not carnal but mighty for pulling down those strongholds that seem to be hurdles in our lives.

> *3For though we walk in the flesh, we do not war according to the flesh. 4For the weapons of our warfare are not [a]carnal but mighty in God for pulling down strongholds, 5casting down arguments and every high thing that exalts itself against the knowledge of God, bringing every thought into captivity to the obedience of Christ. – II Corinthians 10:3-5 (NKJV)*

This is really my weapon that I use to keep standing daily. Think about the hurdles our family has had to face this year. Even our mentor and spiritual father, Bishop Bill Hamon, stated that this year would be a year of transition, change, launching and new beginnings. I could never have known that I would be walking out this prophetic word as we are in the third quarter of this fateful year. However, what a shock as the COVID-19 pandemic settled over not just our country but the entire world. Our family was already dealing with the hurdle of dementia and now we have a pandemic that is producing such fear that people act as though each one has a communicable disease. Who could have imagined that our entire world would be on the same playing field? Schools, businesses, churches, malls, grocery stores, even restaurants shut down for months on end. It did not matter that we had not tested positive for anything. Then our family is faced with divorce, one more hurdle for us to scale because divorce affects the entire family. We certainly did not have death on our calendar, as we expected Henry to live at least another two years.

I want you to realize that our family has been preparing for pandemic our entire lives. We have been ingesting God's Word daily to keep us strong when the battle comes. Out of the entire Bible, I think some of my favorite writings is by Paul, the apostle. This man was probably the most learned student of Biblical history in the Bible and yet he let us know that there were plenty of times that he knew to do right, but he did wrong. His flesh was such an enemy that he had to war with himself to keep standing at times.

For what I am doing, I do not understand. For what I will to do, that I do not practice; but what I hate, that I do. – Romans 7:15 (NKJV)

Doesn't this take away some of the self-judgementalism that we can allow to defeat us daily? Who could have predicted that we, the Jones clan, would be stepping into a new season without Dr. Henry Jones as the head of our family? On those days when I move into the mourning process, I am assisted by the promise in Psalm 30:5 that it will last only momentarily. I refuse to allow a season to determine my lifetime.

For his anger lasts only a moment, but his favor lasts a lifetime! Weeping may last through the night, but joy comes with the morning. – Psalm 30:5

As I walk out this new season with spiritual sons and daughters who have been in our lives for many years, I see the legacy of Henry Jones living out through not only our children and grandchildren but also pastors who are living epistles of the influence of their mentor. Through the years of weekly mentoring and training, Henry was preparing his mentees for the day that he would no longer be there to be their greatest influence. We now laughingly remind each other of certain quotes and instructions that he lived out daily. Because of that influence, we are stronger and motivated to do even more than he accomplished in life. That was his dream.

One of our spiritual daughters informed me that, as they purchase larger office space in this down-sizing world after the pandemic, people are amazed that they are not hesitant to make bold moves. Their answer is that they were taught to walk by faith and not by sight as their spiritual father had done. Henry believed in the kingly-priestly anointing where marketplace and church life should be so interwoven that God's people were receiving the wealth of the wicked which is laid up for the righteous.

One of his favorite sayings was "It's no hill for a climber." I live my life by this saying today. I shall not only walk out my purpose but will undergird those who are walking by my side. Life is not just about me but about everyone that has come along beside me and are stepping into my new season with me.

Made in the USA
Columbia, SC
13 March 2021